JOHN WESLEY'S
Message for
Today

JOHN WESLEY'S
Message for
Today

STEVE HARPER

ZondervanPublishingHouse
Grand Rapids, Michigan

A Division of HarperCollins*Publishers*

JOHN WESLEY'S MESSAGE FOR TODAY, Steve Harper

Copyright © 1983 by The Zondervan Corporation
Grand Rapids, Michigan

Requests for information should be addressed to:
Zondervan Publishing House
Academic and Professional Books
Grand Rapids, Michigan 49530

Library of Congress Cataloging in Publication Data

Harper, Steve.
    John Wesley's message for today.

    Bibliography: p.
    1. Wesley, John, 1703–1791. I. Title.
BX8495.W5H32   1983   230'.7'0924   82-17656
ISBN 0-310-45711-4

Edited by Ben Chapman
Designed by Louise Bauer

Printed in the United States of America

   95 96 97 98 99 00 / DH /20 19 18 17 16 15

Contents

Preface

A genuine renaissance is taking place in Wesley Studies. Christians inside and outside the Wesleyan tradition are studying John Wesley. Outside the tradition he is viewed as a focal point for ecumenical relationships. Inside the tradition he is being taken seriously as a guide to matters of faith and practice. His blend of theology and ministry is attractive. His theology of discipleship fits with the current emphasis on Christian growth and renewal.

I have written this book to help you know John Wesley better. I have shared this material with others and have found many saying, "I've been a Methodist[1] all my life, and I never knew John Wesley believed that!" I have been encouraged by some of these same people to share this kind of information on a wider scale with others. This book is one attempt to get the word out to all who want to become part of the Wesleyan renaissance.

The focus of the book is the "order of salvation," which is discernable in Wesley's theology. Because

---

[1]In this book the term "Methodist" is used in the historic sense. It relates to all subsequent denominations who find their roots in the Wesleyan tradition.

his theology is dynamic, it is important to study any part of it in relation to what precedes and follows it. The order of salvation allows us to do this. It makes possible a study of Wesley's theology *in context*.

However, this book aims to be more than a literal reproduction of eighteenth-century Wesleyan theology. To do that would be to lose the very dynamism Wesley sought for theology. Nothing aggravated him more than "dead orthodoxy." So in this book we are not primarily looking back. Rather, we look to the present (and the future), but we use Wesley's basic *principles* to do it. Admittedly, this is difficult. But it is possible, precisely because Wesley's search was for Scriptural Christianity. To the extent that his theology is Scriptural, it is relevant to our concerns in the twentieth century. Therefore this book speaks to the present, using a time-tested framework.

I have not written for the scholarly community, but, following Wesley's own example, I have sought to use "plain words for plain people." However, I have attempted to document what I have written and refer to primary Wesley material. Only by doing that can the transition be made from history to the present. And only by doing that can I demonstrate a valid consistency with the Wesleyan heritage. The footnotes can serve as useful points of departure for those who want to do more digging; they also serve to anchor the whole work in the foundation of Wesley's own theology.

Because I hope this book will be useful for reflection and study, I have included questions for discussion at the end of each chapter. Also, I have provided suggestions for further reading should you want to explore any area in more detail. You will notice that many of these suggestions are from Wesley's sermons, where the heart of Wesley's theology can be found. He developed his theology not in the ivory tower, but in the marketplace. His theology is life-centered, not idea-saturated. But don't jump to the conclusion that Wesley was not a genuine theologian. It's just that his theology pulsates with life and a concern for the enrichment of life that Christ can give.

Like any book, this one is no individual effort. I must thank several key persons in my life. Untold thanks must go to Dr. Ed Robb for the immeasurable support he has given to my ministry and related scholarly development. Likewise Dr. Frank Baker has multiplied my joy in studying Wesley, given me scholarly tools to do it, and been a continual support as I worked toward a doctorate in Wesley Studies at Duke University. And finally, I express my deep love and appreciation for my wife, Jeannie. Only she knows the sacrifices she has made and the support she has given, all in the spirit of deepest love. Only I know how fortunate I am to have her for my wife.

Meet John Wesley

Wesley offers a treasure to the church of tomorrow that will leave it poorer if ignored.

Albert Outler

1
Meet John Wesley

Meeting John Wesley is like exploring the ocean; there are many ways to do it. You can wade in the shallows or dive in the depths. Either way there is enjoyment and profit. Even after numerous trips you can still return to make new discoveries.

The same is true in coming to know Wesley. It really doesn't matter whether you are seeing him for the first time or the one-hundredth time. Either way your life will be richer. The study of Wesley holds a potential fascination that will keep you returning to him.

And yet, it is an interesting fact that many people who stand in the Wesleyan tradition do not know Wesley himself very well. They are familiar with his heart-warming experience at Aldersgate, but beyond that their knowledge falls off drastically. I have found this to be true among laity and clergy groups. The result is that much of what we label "Wesleyan" is unintelligently associated with that heritage, and sometimes what is included in the Wesleyan tradition is not true to Wesley at all.

Who is John Wesley? Can we meet him? Will that meeting make any difference in our Christian lives?

On the biographical level it is helpful to mention some basic facts.[1] He was born on 17 June, 1703, the fifteenth child and second surviving son of Samuel and Susanna Wesley. His early life in Epworth was largely shaped by the example of his parents and in particular the educational program Susanna operated in the rectory.

When he was six, he was rescued from the burning rectory in so remarkable a fashion that Susanna believed the hand of God was upon him in a special way. Accordingly, she felt a particular responsibility to nurture the life of her son. What she did had its lifelong effects. And even today John Wesley's life at Epworth is rightly considered the "cradle of Methodism."[2]

In 1713 Wesley moved to London to attend Charterhouse School. In comparison to other periods in his life, his years at Charterhouse were of lesser significance. However, while there he continued to read his Bible and say his prayers daily.[3] After six years at Charterhouse he matriculated to Christ Church College at Oxford where he received the Bachelor of Arts degree in 1726.

Wesley's early Oxford years saw the beginning of his spiritual pilgrimage. In 1725, after reading Jeremy Taylor's *Holy Living* and Thomas á Kempis's *Imitation of Christ*, he resolved to dedicate his life to

---

[1] If you have not done so, it would be well to read a biography of Wesley. Two recent ones are Stanley Ayling's *John Wesley* (New York: Collins, 1979) and Robert Tuttle's *John Wesley: His Life and Theology* (Grand Rapids: Zondervan, 1978).

[2] Martin Schmidt, *John Wesley: A Theological Biography* (Nashville: Abingdon, 1962), 1:63.

[3] Thomas Jackson (ed), *The Works of John Wesley* (Grand Rapids: Baker, 1979), 1:98.

God.[4] The next thirteen years were an agonizing attempt to work out the implications of that resolution. However, it all came together in the now-famous Aldersgate experience on 24 May, 1738. There Wesley found the personal assurance necessary to give life and power to his faith.

From this point onward Wesley became England's greatest preacher and organizer; multitudes responded to his preaching, and he sought to nurture them through the United Societies, which he organized. The last sixty years of his life were a constant motion of traveling and preaching that took him over 250,000 miles (mostly on horseback) and gave him the opportunity of preaching over 44,000 times. Erwin Paul Rudolph has commented that, "In Wesley's work we see the figure of a great preacher, an untiring worker, and a popular but autocratic leader. He reveals a mind that is shrewd, but capable of humor, and that is filled with the sense of divine mission."[5]

Wesley rested from his labors on 2 March, 1791. His last words served not only to capture the quality of life he lived, but also the kind of life he wished for others. He died saying, "The best of all is, God is with us!"

While these facts are important, they do not fully capture Wesley, the man. There are other qualities we should be familiar with if we are to "meet John Wesley" in these opening pages. For me, the most appealing thing about him is that he is a fellow pilgrim in the faith. He was in search of vital faith

---

[4]Jackson, *Works*, 11:366–67.
[5]Erwin P. Rudolph, *The John Wesley Treasury* (Wheaton: Victor Books, 1979), p. 11.

just as we are. When you read his diary, journal, and letters, this comes through loud and clear. He faced struggles similar to ours. He made his share of mistakes. He asked questions during times of doubt and depression. He knew the elation of victory. In a very real sense, Wesley was one of us.

Furthermore, Wesley was a *practical theologian.* This does not mean that he was unfamiliar with theology on a scholarly level, or that he could not handle himself with the so-called theological heavyweights of his day. One reading of his *Appeals to Men of Reason and Religion* is sufficient to dispel that notion.[6] What it does mean is that Wesley was primarily concerned about developing a faith that worked in everyday living. He was in search of a "Scriptural Christianity" that was confirmed by human experience. The fact that his theology is biblical gives it a timelessness; the fact that it is confirmed by experience gives it an authenticity that theology in the ivory tower sometimes lacks. Wesley's theology has been road tested, and found effective.

To know Wesley is also to know a person of intense and meaningful discipline. Every day counted; every moment was a "God-moment." Consequently, he gave himself daily to the spiritual disciplines of prayer, Bible study, and devotion. But discipline was never an end in itself. It was the means to a vital relationship with God and the resulting power that comes from that relationship.

As the Methodist movement began to grow, Wesley sought to instill this same spirit of discipline

---

6Jackson, *Works,* 8:3–247.

into his followers. The bands, classes, and societies
were all organized on explicit disciplinary principles.[7] Members were held accountable for living up
to the disciplines. And through the sense of personal
and corporate discipline early Methodism had both a
vitality and a stability that some contemporary
church life fails to exhibit. To know Wesley is to
know one who echoes the saying, "The soul and the
body make the man; and the spirit and discipline
make a Christian."[8]

As you read this book, keep in mind the word
"daily." Wesley's life and theology pulsate with this
word. For over sixty years he faithfully engaged in
devotional *living*. He calls us to do the same. He
challenges us to break out of any compartmentalized
concept of Christianity. Jesus is Lord! Every moment
is tc be lived in his presence. While we may not
exactly duplicate his methods, we should strive to
imitate his discipline.

Knowing John Wesley requires that we see him
in a community sense. Wesley was a churchman in
the highest and best sense of the term. This is important to see early in this book. Too often he is cast
in the light of a malcontent just looking for a good
reason to start a new church. Never forget that he
lived *and died* an Anglican. He did not inaugurate a
new denomination and he discouraged his followers
from doing so.[9] In the very first annual conference
that Wesley held in 1744, he declared his allegiance

---

[7]Jackson, *Works,* 7:248–388.

[8]Ibid., 13:101.

[9]The issue here is complex. The best interpretation I have
found is Frank Baker's *John Wesley and the Church of England*
(Nashville: Abingdon, 1970).

to the Anglican Church and exhorted the Methodists to constant attendance of "both the word preached and the sacraments administered therein."[10] And throughout his lifetime, Methodism was a renewal movement within the larger Anglican Church.[11]

Having said this, it is equally important to stress that Wesley's ultimate loyalty was to God. As much as he loved the Anglican Church, he loved God more. Where he felt the church had strayed, he stood against it. He was a true "son of the Reformation." The point to be stressed in all this is that his disagreements with the Church of England were not institutional, they were Scriptural. He felt that eighteenth-century Anglicanism had drifted from important Scriptural norms[12], and he viewed the Methodist movement as simply describing "the plain, old religion of the Church of England."[13] His goal was not defection, but rather renewal. His constant prayer was that the renewal could take place *within* Anglicanism. That it did not is a fact of church history, not a fact Wesley's design. To know Wesley is to know a churchman.

Because his churchmanship was based on Scripture rather than contemporary doctrinal formulations[14] his theology has a dynamism. He abhored

___

[10]Jackson, *Works*, 8:280.

[11]More will be said on Wesley's theology of the church in chapter 9.

[12]eg., justification by faith, new birth, repentance in believers, entire sanctification, et al.

[13]Jackson, *Works*, 1:232.

[14]He fully accepted and took seriously the Anglican *Articles of Religion* and the *Homilies*. In fact, he considered them more authoritative than some of his contemporaries did. But he did so on the basis of his conviction that they were reflections of Scriptural truth.

stagnant orthodoxy.[15] He sought a Scriptural Christianity "energized" by the ongoing presence of the
Holy Spirit. While his theology comes from the
eighteenth century, it is not bound by it. Furthermore, it moves in harmony with Christian experience. In his preface to the Standard Sermons he
wrote, "I want to know one thing—the way to
heaven."[16] For Wesley, that "way" was dynamic,
moving from sin to glorification. I have tried to capture this feature of Wesley's theology in this book by
basing the chapters on the "order of salvation" that
emerges in his writings. Wesley never produced a
systematic theology in the formal sense, but what he
did produce is systematic and consistent. I hope that
the organization of this book will help you know
Wesley in that light.

Finally, to know Wesley is to know someone
you can read and understand. By his own design he
avoided complex theological terminology. He wrote,
"I desire plain truth for plain people; therefore, of set
purpose, I abstain from all nice and philosophical
speculations."[17] As previously noted, he could deal
with theology on a sophisticated level when he
needed to. But in the general course of his ministry
he desired to communicate with ordinary people in
understandable ways. If you have previously shied
away from reading theology, you are in for a pleasant
surprise in Wesley. His simplicity will not insult
your intelligence, it will increase it. His life-cen-
teredness will touch you where you live, and cause

---

[15]Jackson, *Works*, 5:78.
[16]John Wesley, *Forty Four Sermons* (London: Epworth
Press, 1944), p. vi. Cf. Jackson, *Works*, 5:3.
[17]Jackson, *Works*, 5:2.

you to consider your own beliefs and actions. This is the kind of experience I hope you will have as you read this book. It is the kind of experience Wesley would wish for you.

I trust that this chapter has helped you sense something of a kinship with John Wesley. Such a kinship will enrich your reading of the following material. In fact, the following chapters cannot be read in a detached manner. Wesley would not only want you to understand his message, he would want you to be affected by it. He would want you to experience the Christ to whom it points. Time and time again Wesley wrote that he "offered Christ." Through this reconstruction of Wesley's message, he is offering Christ to you again!

For Discussion

1. Does your experience confirm (or deny) the author's assertion that even people in the Wesleyan tradition do not know Wesley very well? If you are not in the Wesleyan tradition, how well do people in your tradition know him?

2. Among the various features of Wesley's life and theology, which was the most attractive to you? Why?

3. What are your desires and dreams as you begin this book? What do you hope it will do for you?

For Further Reading

Albert Outler, *John Wesley* (New York: Oxford, 1964).

Skevington Wood, *John Wesley, The Burning Heart* (Kansas City: Beacon Hill, 1977).

The Root
of the Problem
(Original Sin)

The doctrine of universal sinfulness, concludes Wesley, constitutes the fundamental difference between Christianity and Heathenism.

Martin Schmidt

2
The Root of the Problem
(Original Sin)

Y ou don't have to be a Christian to realize something is wrong with the human race. Our most
brilliant social analysts stand amazed in the presence of radical, often unpredictable experiences of
man's inhumanity to man. Politicians all over the
world are calling for the upholding of basic human
rights. All the while an ominous nuclear cloud
hangs overhead, reminding us that the entire destruction of this planet is possible. Everyone seems
to be asking, "What is wrong?"

When John Wesley looked at his century, he
asked the same question. He concluded that the fundamental problem was human sinfulness. Interestingly, this side of Wesley is often overshadowed by
his emphasis on love. While it is true that he stressed
God's love as a major plank in his theology, it is also
true that he was aware of the dangers when love is
emphasized to the neglect of other things. In a letter
to Joseph Cownley Wesley made the point clear:

> Is it not most pleasing to me as well as
> to you to be always preaching of the love
> of God?. . . . But yet it would be utterly

wrong and unscriptural to preach of
nothing else. . . . The bulk of our hearers
must be purged before they are fed; else
we only feed the disease. Beware of all
honey. It is the best extreme, but it is an
extreme.[1]

This statement makes it clear that Wesley's theology of love was not sentimentalism. It was love
based on at least two primary considerations. First,
Wesley believed that God loved man as the supreme
object of his creation. Wesley believed in the original
righteousness of man.[2] He expressed this belief
using the words of another, "With the same breath
that God breathed into him a living soul, he breathed
into him a righteous soul. This righteousness was
the conformity of all the faculties and powers of his
soul to the moral law."[3] A belief in original righteousness gave Wesley the primary reason for him to
believe in God's love.

But secondly, it was love expressed in the midst
of human sin. In his *Notes Upon the New Testament*
Wesley affirmed the universality of sin in relation to
human nature, temper, and action.[4] No part of man's
existence escaped the contamination. This view gave
Wesley's theology of love an authentic substance. It
was love offered in the face of rejection. It was not
love expressed in the hope of getting something in

[1]John Telford (ed.), *The Letters of John Wesley* (London:
Epworth Press, 1960), 3:34.
[2]Jackson, *Works*, 9:339–53; 435.
[3]*Ibid.*, p. 435. Wesley is quoting from Boston's *Fourfold
State of Man.*
[4]John Wesley, *Explanatory Notes Upon the New Testament*
(Naperville, IL: Alec R. Allenson, 1966), p. 530. (Rom. 3:23)

return,[5] rather it was love expressed where rebellion and even hatred seemed to have won the day.

So the first step in understanding Wesley is to understand the depth and tragedy of human sinfulness. Wesley said it himself, "We know no gospel without salvation from sin."[6] Such a serious view of sin is to be reckoned with in an age when some theologians are inclined to paint a picture of love that minimizes or ignores the fact of universal human sinfulness. Wesley cannot be read or interpreted in this light. His proclamation of great love must always be seen against the backdrop of deep need.

But what is sin? Again, we must pause to get our bearings. For Wesley, sin was not some mysterious spiritual entity which attached itself to human nature like a barnacle attaches itself to the hull of a ship. Instead, Wesley spoke of sin in relational terms. His classic definition is that sin is "every voluntary breach of the law of love."[7] At its base sin is broken relationship, whether that brokenness is expressed toward others or toward God. And it is important to note that the breach is conscious and willful. For Wesley, sin is not something that sneaks up on you, it arises out of you.

The result of sin is sickness. One of Wesley's favorite terms is "corruption." Because of sin humanity is sick unto death. Wesley's definition of sin involves a cause and effect relationship. The cause is

---

[5] This is the basis upon which much human love is founded. The amazing thing about God's love is that it is offered with no strings attached. God loves even when no love is returned!

[6] Telford, *Letters*, 6:327.

[7] Ibid., p. 322.

willful transgression, the result is sickness. And the disease of sin has "spread itself over the whole man, leaving no part uninfected."[8] This means that sin goes deeper than any acts we commit. The Bible does not say we are sinners because we commit acts of sin, it says we commit acts of sin because we are sinners. Sin has struck at the root of what it means to be human.

Wesley believed that Adam was in a perfect state before the Fall. He bore the image of God completely as God had intended it to be borne. But in the Fall something happened. The "imago dei" was *radically* damaged. The moral aspects of the image were lost.[9] The natural aspects of the image were extensively marred but not completely destroyed. Humanity retained some degree of rationality, emotion, and will, but because they were severely tainted they served to increase the overall curse. Man was unable to come to God using these faculties alone. In short, the life of God in the soul of man was virtually extinguished. Wesley put it this way, "The glory departed from him."[10] Intimacy between God and man was gone. Separation was the result. Spiritual sickness unto death was the condition.

This kind of thinking cuts across the grain of much thinking today. Some in our society deny the objective reality of sin altogether. Others try to explain it philosophically as the absence of goodness.

---

[8]Wesley, *Notes Upon the New Testament*, p. 540. (Rom. 6:6)

[9]Wesley included righteousness and true holiness in his understanding of the "moral image."

[10]Jackson, *Works*, 6:272 (sermon: "The End of Christ's Coming").

More often the idea itself is softened under the term "mistake" or the phrase, "nobody's perfect." So it may well be that this kind of view will take some getting used to. But it did in Wesley's day, too. He wrote, "It is now quite unfashionable to say anything to the disparagement of human nature."[11]

However, the eighteenth century's naïve optimism did not prevent Wesley from proclaiming the picture as he saw it. It must not stop us either. We need a fresh affirmation of the reality and danger of sin, not from the standpoint of pessimism, but from the perspective of realism. For you see, we need a Savior only if we need saving; we need a Savior only if we cannot save ourselves. This is precisely what Wesley calls us to acknowledge in his doctrine of sin.

Wesley drove his point home even more by stressing the universality of sin. He not only spoke of sin's nature, he also made it clear that everyone has been infected. All have sinned. He did not try to spell out how we share in Adam's original sin, he simply said that in some way we all died in Adam.[12] For evidence he turned not to speculation, but to human conduct.

Even here Wesley was not content to point his finger at the "gross sinners" whom everyone would recognize to be such. He called on decent people to repent and be saved. He knew that one might live an outwardly respectable life and still be lost. Anyone, gross or respectable, who lived as if God did not matter illustrated the universality of sin. This kind of

---

[11]Jackson, *Works*, p. 55 (sermon: "Original Sin").
[12]Ibid., p. 68 (sermon: "The New Birth").

sin runs silent and deep. It takes no holidays. It leaves no one immune. One of Wesley's favorite texts was Genesis 6:5, which speaks about man's heart being *continually* set on evil. In more poetic fashion, his brother Charles described this as humanity's "bent to sinning."[13]

What are the implications of this doctrine? Simply this: if sin were a "thing", we might find some way to rid ourselves of it or cut it off, etc. But because it is an infection of our humanity, the only option is transformation. We cannot try hard enough, learn enough, worship enough, or work enough to heal ourselves. Outside help is the only possible solution.

I read about a man who went into the desert to live as a hermit. He reasoned that by doing so he could remove himself from "this sinful world." But he did not stay long, and when he returned he said, "I could not run away from sin, because it was in me. Everywhere I went, there I was." I heard of a woman who frantically approached an airline ticket counter, placed several hundred dollars on the counter and said, "Use this and send me anywhere you can and back in three days. I cannot stand it here another minute."

We eventually come to see that the problem of sin is a problem infecting the very nature of what it means to be human. Any attempts to remove ourselves from it are only exercises in futility. The solution is transformation, not escape. Wesley can help us out of our futile efforts to treat sin as a "thing." He

---

[13]Taken from Charles Wesley's hymn, "Love Divine All Love Excelling."

can help us by reminding us that at its heart, sin is disease. Healing is the only solution.

This is the nature of sin in Wesley's theology. It is only natural to assume that anything this pervasive would have certain effects. Wesley spoke to some of these effects in his writings. For one thing, he said that sin makes us dead toward God. He spoke of the Fall as having brought death to the soul.[14] The irony of this soul death is that it gives a false sense of security and peace. Wesley put it this way. "The poor unawakened sinner has no knowledge of himself. He knows not that he is a fallen spirit. Full of diseases as he is, he fancies himself in perfect health."[15]

Even more dangerous is that soul death is a very active state. Wesley compared spiritual death to the branches that spring out of an evil root. The branches produce the fruit of unbelief, independence, pride, vanity, ambition, covetousness, lust, anger, envy, and sorrow.[16] Wesley went on to say that this condition, if left untreated, would evolve into eternal death.

Another effect of sin is self-captivity. For Wesley this was the logical consequence of being dead to God. If one is truly dead to God, then the only alternative is to turn inward and make self a "god." Wesley saw humanity doing just that, and doing it in the name of freedom. Ironically this so-called freedom was the worst form of slavery. Needing a perspective on life greater than his own, man was trapped by the limits of his own reason. Needing a power beyond himself,

[14]Jackson, *Works*, 5:54 (sermon: "Justification By Faith").
[15]Ibid., p. 26 (sermon: "Awake, Thou That Sleepest").
[16]Ibid., pp. 82–84 (sermon: "The Way to the Kingdom").

he found himself prey to his own weakness. As someone put it, "I may be the captain of my soul, but I keep driving myself around in circles."

A third effect of sin is helplessness to change. Even though Wesley did not believe in the total destruction of the image of God, he did believe it had been rendered powerless to revitalize itself. Even a person under conviction was in need of grace to find victory. Wesley described this dilemma by saying, "Now he truly desires to break loose from sin and begins to struggle with it. But though he strive with all his might, he cannot conquer; sin is mightier than he."[17]

I have always been fascinated with those who call Christianity a crutch, or who claim it is for weak people. They would opt for an unrealistic optimism in human ability—a bootstrap theology—self-helpism. If such a person were to approach Wesley and say, "Christianity is for weak people," he would reply, "Correct! And we are all weak!" We cannot pull ourselves up by our own bootstraps. Grace is essential.

It is at this very point that Wesley's theology of sin evolves into the proclamation of the Good News. He never spoke of sin's nature or its effects without also speaking of the remedy. There is power for the powerless. There is help for the helpless. There is a cure for the disease. One of his favorite texts was, "Here is a trustworthy saying that deserves full acceptance: Christ Jesus came into the world to save sinners." (1 Timothy 1:15) God took the initiative.

---

[17]Jackson, *Works*, p. 104 (sermon: "The Spirit of Bondage and the Spirit of Adoption").

He sought us. He provided the healing medicine. In the following chapters we will see how God effects that healing. For now it is enough to know that in Christ there is deliverance and healing.

This has not been an easy chapter to write; by today's standards it seems pessimistic. But that is only because the contemporary view of man is overly optimistic. By avoiding a biblical view of sin we have failed to come to grips with the reality and extent of it. Wesley's view was not meant to depress people or to send them on guilt trips. Rather, it was meant to awaken them, to bring them to a realistic awareness of their condition. He felt that only then could a person adequately deal with sin. Wesley attacks expressions of self-sufficiency in order that we may fall back upon the necessity of God's grace. Wesley's last word is one of hope, victory, and triumph.

Charles Wesley captured the theme of triumph over sin in his classic hymn, *And Can It Be*. Through these words we may hear the voice of God:

> Long my imprisoned spirit lay
> Fast bound by sin and nature's night
> Thine eye diffused a quickening ray,
> I woke, the dungeon flamed with light.
> My chains fell off, my heart was free.
> I rose, went forth, and followed thee!

For Discussion

1. What evidence do you see in contemporary living that we have sentimentalized love?

2. How do you see the universality of sin illustrated today?

3. What does Wesley's view of sin have to offer those who are tempted to despair over the condition of their lives?

4. Think of your own experience. In what ways did God take the initiative to bring you to acknowledge your helplessness?

For Further Reading

Sermon, "Original Sin" Works, 6:54–64.

Sermon, "On the Fall of Man" Works, 6:215–24.

Sermon, "The Way to the Kingdom" Works, 5:76–86

The Power
to Begin
(Prevenient Grace)

Wesley's theological system builds on the doctrine of original sin and prevenient grace.

Robert Tuttle

3
The Power to Begin
(Prevenient Grace)

I f an artist were to paint a picture of John Wesley's doctrine of sin, he might portray a person hopelessly lost on the sea. He would capture the struggle and agony on the face of the person. He would show the utter despair of the situation. The painting would carry this unwritten message: "There is nothing this man can do to save himself. Outside help is his only hope."

At this point the artist would have a problem. He would be faced with the task of adding another dimension to the work. He would have to find a way of including the presence and reality of that "outside help." To be true to Wesley he would have to show that God has broken through into the hopelessness. In theological terms he would have to portray the idea of *prevenient grace*.

For many the idea of prevenient grace is a new idea. Even some in the Wesleyan tradition are not familiar with the term. But it is crucial in understanding Wesley's order of salvation. Failure to include it has led some to erroneously conclude that Wesley believed in natural human ability and complete freedom of the will. But as we shall see, this is not Wesley's position.

Before we look at prevenient grace in particular, I believe it is important to speak of grace in general. Grace is grace. You do not have one kind of grace for one situation and another kind for some other situation. By the same token God does not give his grace in bits and pieces. We define grace in different ways because of how we experience the grace on our end of the relationship. Grace comes to us at different stages in our spiritual pilgrimage, and it accomplishes different effects and evokes different responses. But it is all grace.

When Wesley spoke of prevenient grace he meant the grace of God which operates before our experience of conversion.[1] It is his term for the grace of God that is active before we give conscious thought to God or our need of him. To use biblical language, it is the grace that comes while we are "still sinners" (Rom. 5:8). In Wesley's theology this action of grace is particularly important, and we need to work through it carefully.

We must begin with the definition alluded to in the previous paragraph. Literally, prevenient grace means "the grace that comes before."[2] Before what? Before any *conscious* personal experience of divine grace. Through his doctrine of prevenient grace Wesley was saying that the first move is God's, not man's. Without this Wesley said we might have some room for boasting. Prevenient grace removes

---

[1] Jackson, *Works*, 6:511–13 (sermon: "On Working Out Our Own Salvation").

[2] John Lawson, *Introduction to Christian Doctrine* (Wilmore, Kentucky: Asbury, 1980). p. 214.

"all imagination of merit from man."[3] But even more to the point is the impossibility of man to come to God on his own. Wesley stated it plainly: "It is not possible for men to do anything well till God raises them from the dead . . . It is impossible for us to come out of our sins, yea, or to make the least motion toward it, till He who hath all power in heaven and earth call our dead souls into life."[4]

This should lay to rest once and for all any notions that Wesley believed in natural human ability. He said it plainly, "all men are by nature not only sick, but 'dead in trespasses and sins.'"[5] The doctrine of prevenient grace means that God takes the first step to redeem humanity. And for Wesley, he allows this grace to operate in and through the human conscience.

He disliked the term "natural conscience," which was used in his day. He believed that while every man had a conscience, it was placed there as a supernatural gift of God.[6] His favorite text to illustrate this truth was John 1:9 where the preincarnate Word of God is said to be "the true light that gives light to every man." Clearly Wesley saw prevenient grace as the activity of God before conversion, totally apart from man's ability or initiative.

Additionally, prevenient grace is "leading grace." It is the operation of God that moves us to the place of repentance. Wesley indicated three ways in which prevenient grace "leads" us. First, it creates in us our first sensitivity to God's will. Second, it pro-

---

[3]Jackson, *Works*, 6:508.
[4]Ibid., p. 511.
[5]Ibid.
[6]Ibid., p. 509.

duces a slight, even transient conviction of having violated His will. And third, it causes our first wish to please God.[7] Through these experiences Wesley believed a person would be led to the place of repentance, which was itself a step along the way to full salvation.

It is important to emphasize that prevenient grace is not sufficient for salvation. If a person chooses to ignore or suppress this grace, he will experience hardness of heart so that these stirrings of God will go unheeded. Nevertheless, because prevenient grace is involved in moving a person to the place of repentance, Wesley included it in his overall scheme of salvation. All the while he was giving priority to the activity of God. He put it this way: "God worketh in you; therefore you can work. Otherwise it would be impossible."[8] Like all other aspects of grace, prevenient grace is a gift; in this light, two other facts emerge.

First, it is grace *for all*. No one is excluded from the operation of prevenient grace. Wesley would echo the apostle Peter who said that God is "not wanting anyone to perish, but everyone to come to repentance" (2 Pet. 3:9). Second, it is grace *in all*. It is only because of grace that anything resembling the image of God remains in us. Were it not for grace we would have been stripped of anything good, noble, just, or pure. This means that we do not merely live in an atmosphere of grace; it means that the life we now live is due to the grace of God!

This is Wesley's doctrine of prevenient grace

---

[7]Jackson, *Works*, p. 509.
[8]Ibid., p. 511.

viewed from a theological perspective. But how does it work "in us" from a more practical point of view? What happens to the person under the influence of prevenient grace? Wesley gave a twofold answer. First, prevenient grace works to create *awareness*. It awakens us to God and our need of salvation. Wesley believed we were awakened either by natural revelation or the operation of the Law. God has left his footprints in creation. He is not contained in creation or equated with it, but he is revealed by it. Wesley believed that if any thoughtful person considered the beauty and complexity of the universe, he would have to consider the possibility of God's existence. There is too much around us that speaks of Someone greater than ourselves. And he also believed that if a person believed in the possibility of God, he would realize that if God exists, he matters completely. If God exists, the rest of life is defined in terms of him. If God exists, life is lived in relation to him. Through natural revelation these kinds of thoughts come to mind.

Wesley also believed that prevenient grace operated through the Law. He said, "It is the ordinary method of the Spirit of God to convict sinners by the Law."[9] The Law brings knowledge of God's will. With that knowledge we are able to see which side of the fence we are on. Through the Law we are able to see that we have fallen short of the glory of God. And out of this knowledge can flow a sense of need. We see ourselves as we really are. Our consciences are stirred.[10]

---

[9]Jackson, *Works*, 5:443 (sermon: "The Original Nature, Property, and Use of the Law").

[10]Ibid., 7:187 (sermon: "On Conscience").

But Wesley knew that knowledge alone is not enough. Bare knowledge does not contain the power to change. In fact, knowledge without power leads to despair. We have all felt the frustration of knowing more than we were living up to. So Wesley knew that the will had to be brought into the picture. We change by action of the will. Therefore, prevenient grace operates in the second major way to give us "response-ability."

Here is an important point in Wesleyan theology. We have been told in Christianity that we are responsible for the sins we commit. Wesley saw that this could not be so if God had irrevocably decreed our destiny before the foundation of the world. Absolute decree undercuts authentic responsibility. Wesley taught that we can be held accountable only if we have genuine power of choice. He believed that prevenient grace enabled us to exercise our wills. *Through grace* we can be truly responsible!

There is risk here. If God has given us the power to choose through prevenient grace, He runs the risk of our choosing against Him. But Wesley believed that wherever love was in operation risk was always present. Love must be freely given and freely received. We have no problem in seeing God's free gift of love in Jesus Christ. Wesley wants us to see that our response to that gift is also free. In that kind of freedom there can be authentic relationship.

God has taken the risk. By his grace he has enabled us to respond. Everyone is included in the *offer* of salvation. No one is inescapably trapped in sin. No one is destined to Hell because of the action of God. On the contrary, God is at work to win as many as possible to Himself. Even in the darkest night of the soul there can be the dawning of light. It is light that points toward a door—a Way. It speaks to us in the sickness and paralyzing grip of sin and says, "Rise, take up your bed, and walk!"

If you have read this chapter as a Christian, you will be able to look into your past and see many of the ways God's prevenient grace operated in your life to bring you to the place of commitment. If you are reading this chapter as a non-Christian, you too will be able to reflect on those experiences that have shed "light" on your path. All of these experiences are examples of prevenient grace. The challenge is to act in accordance with what you have received and to respond to God if you will.

The message of prevenient grace is a message of hope. There is a way out of the human dilemma. There is a way out of our problems. God has made the way! And by his prevenient grace he enables us to walk in that way if we choose to do so. Prevenient grace is not the whole story, but it is the beginning. It is not the bright light of day, but it is the first light of dawn. It is real light, light enough to see the hand of God and to reach for it.

For Discussion

1. As you think of your experience, what events in your past before conversion would you consider activities of God's prevenient grace?

2. Do you agree that knowledge alone (without the power to change) is not sufficient? Are there any experiences in your life where this has been so?

3. How do you react to the statement that God holds us personally responsible only if we are able to respond? How does prevenient grace operate to make us truly responsible?

For Further Reading

Sermon, "Justification By Faith," Works, 5:53–64.

Sermon, "The Witness of the Spirit," Works, 5:134–43.

Sermon, "On Conscience," Works, 7:186–94.

Sermon, "On Working Out Our Own Salvation," Works, 6:506–13.

The Turning Point (Converting Grace)

It is by grace of God that man turns, but he turns!

Frederick Norwood

4

The Turning Point
(Converting Grace)

Light has broken through into the darkness! God
has entered the human scene, made us aware of
our condition, and offered us a way out. This is the
first step in Wesley's understanding of the gospel.
But he did not stop here. He knew that prevenient
grace was only the first light of dawn in the soul. It
was a guide, which if accepted, would lead a person
to the brink of saving grace. Whenever Wesley spoke
of prevenient grace, he encouraged his hearers to
"stir up the spark of grace which is now in you, and
God will give you more grace."[1] In this chapter we
will consider the next step in the activity of grace.
We will explore what John Wesley called "saving
grace."

Whenever we speak of salvation, we are describing an experience that has two sides—a divine
side and a human side. From the divine side, salvation is by grace *alone*. As Wesley put it, "There is
nothing we are, or have, or do, which can deserve the
least thing at God's hand."[2] St. Paul expressed it this

---

[1]Jackson, *Works,* 6:513 (sermon: "Working Out Our Own
Salvation").

[2]Ibid., 5:7 (sermon: "Salvation by Faith").

way, "For it is by grace you have been saved" (Eph. 2:8). It is only by divine action that anyone is saved. But God has acted! Through Christ justice has been done and grace has been given. Mercy has triumphed over condemnation. We have been saved *by grace!*

From the human side, salvation is by faith. Paul goes on to say, "For it is by grace you have been saved, *through faith.*" Faith is the human response to divine grace. It is our reaction to God's prior action. But even faith is not of ourselves. It too is the gift of God, which he gives to us through prevenient grace. Prevenient grace enables us to make a faith response. So while faith issues from us, it does not originate in us.

For Wesley, the faith response was characterized by two movements: repentance and belief. Taken together, these constitute "saving faith." Wesley is clearly one with the biblical revelation. Both John the Baptist and Jesus began their public ministries with the call to repent (Matt. 3:2, 4:17). When Paul defended his ministry before King Agrippa, he declared that his message was that people "should repent and turn to God" (Acts 26:20). When Wesley proclaimed the message of saving grace, he focused on the same terms: *repent* and *believe.*

But what does it mean to repent? Unfortunately, some people associate it with negative images. Others identify it with going to an altar. Still others view it primarily in terms of sorrow. However, when the New Testament speaks of repentance, it uses the basic idea of change. Wesley called it, "a change of heart from all sin to all holiness."[3] He meant that

---

[3]Wesley, *Notes Upon the New Testament*, (Matt. 3:8).

whereas we once lived in sin with little thought of God, now we have had a change of mind. Now we know that sin matters; it must be forsaken. Now we know that God matters. He must be followed. We have made a 180-degree turn. Tears may or may not be involved. An altar may be the place of repentance, but so may our living room at home. In either state or location the principle remains; we have changed. And Wesley believed this change would affect us in several ways.

First, we change in the knowledge of ourselves. We now see ourselves as living apart from God. Wesley urged his followers "Know thyself to be a sinner. Know that corruption of thy inmost nature. Know that thou art corrupted in every power."[4] In repentance we have a change of heart about our spiritual condition. Apart from God we are not "O.K." We are in a desperate condition. Wesley calls us to see ourselves realistically. This is the first effect of repentance.

Second, we experience further change through conviction. When we realize the true condition of our lives apart from God, we are pricked in our hearts. Wesley believed that in conviction God impressed upon our minds the fact of our guilt and our deserving eternal destruction.[5] Such a self-understanding would weigh heavy upon us. But while the picture is unpleasant, Wesley never intended it to be negative. Rather, conviction was viewed as a part of God's *positive* action in our lives.

Unfortunately, we have often pictured convic-

---

[4]Jackson, *Works,* 5:82 (sermon: "The Way to the Kingdom").
[5]Ibid., p. 81.

tion in negative images. We have used it to create guilt feelings in our hearers. To some it means primarily that we have finally been caught. When conviction is expressed in these ways, it is viewed as something to get away from, something to be thrown off—like getting out from under a spiritual hornets' nest. On the contrary, the truer picture is that conviction indicates our hearts are still sensitive enough for God's Spirit to touch them. It is proof positive that our souls are still open enough for the risen Christ to enter. Conviction is a positive experience, although it may be unpleasant. It is the "warning light of the soul" that lets us know that all is not well. Adjustments need to be made.

In non-Christians conviction works to bring them to the place of salvation. As a surgeon's knife must cut before it can cure, so conviction must come before we can find victory over sin. But conviction is not limited to those outside the faith. Christians continue to be convicted as the Holy Spirit prompts us to make midcourse corrections. In this dimension Wesley recognized the need for repentance in believers.

Third, repentance includes a thorough change of our minds.[6] This is the true end of repentance. It is illustrated most perfectly in the story of the prodigal son in Luke 15. After the younger son left home, his condition deteriorated rapidly. He ended up in the pigpen. While there he came to a new self-understanding. He saw the contrast of life there and life at home. Self-knowledge led to the conviction that he had sinned, and that he should return home. So far,

---

[6]Jackson, Works, p. 83.

so good. But if he had stopped there, he would have
stayed in the pigpen forever. Another step was
needed. He had to engage his will. He needed to act
upon his conviction. The process of repentance was
completed when he said, "I will set out and go back
to my father."

Repentance climaxes in the determination to go
home. The step has to be taken, or else all the self-
knowledge and conviction in the world will not
suffice. Wesley is scriptural and realistic in calling
for action in repentance. We need to be changed.
And repentance calls for change.

Before leaving the matter of repentance, it is important to note that Wesley believed repentance
comes before true belief. In a sermon he said,

> We must repent before we can believe
> the gospel. We must be cut off from de-
> pendency upon ourselves before we can
> truly depend on Christ. We must cast
> away all confidence in our own right-
> eousness, or we cannot have a true
> confidence in his. Till we are delivered
> from trusting in anything that we do, we
> cannot thoroughly trust in what he has
> done and suffered. First, we receive the
> sentence of death in ourselves: then, we
> trust in him that lived and died for us.[7]

But even repentance is not the end of the process. Wesley called repentance "the porch of religion."[8] The second major part of saving grace is
faith. Wesley knew it is not sufficient to get away

---

[7]Jackson, *Works*, 5:241 (sermon: "The Lord Our Righteousness").

[8]Telford, *Letters*, 2:268.

from the problem. We must move toward the solution. It is not sufficient to turn *from* something; we must turn *toward* Someone.

Jesus taught this clearly in Matthew 12. He told of the person who had an evil spirit. The person "cleaned house" and was rid of the demon. The old was gone. The life was cleaned up and aired out. But it was empty. One day the evil spirit strolled by and noticed the house. It was in better shape than ever! The demon had an idea. He went and called seven of his friends, and they all went and entered into the person's life. Jesus said the end result was worse than the first. Why? Because he had only gone halfway. The old was gone, but he had not embraced the new. In his emptiness, he was vulnerable.

The same is true in the process of saving grace. Repentance is not enough. It is like one act of a two act drama. Act two is necessary to complete the play. Act two is *belief*. Because this is a common term in Christianity, it is necessary to see what Wesley meant by it.

It is clear what he did *not* mean. He did not mean mere intellectual assent to a creed or statement of faith. He did not mean only the rational activity of the mind. He said,

> Only beware thou dost not deceive thy own soul, with regard to the nature of this faith. It is not, as some have fondly conceived, a bare assent to the truth of the Bible, or the articles of our creed, or of all that is contained in the Old and New Testaments. The devils believe this . . . and yet they are devils still.[9]

9Jackson, *Works,* 5:85 (sermon: "The Way to the Kingdom").

The preceding remarks should not be taken to mean that Wesley minimized the intellectual dimension of faith. His own life disproves that. He sought whenever possible to have a reasonable faith. But it does mean that he knew that belief, in the scriptural sense, involved much more. He included at least four strands in his understanding of it.

First, belief means to put your confidence and trust in the mercy and forgiveness of God. Wesley put it this way, "To believe in God implies, to trust in him as our strength, without whom we can do nothing . . . as our help, our only help in time of trouble."[10] Through prevenient grace we see the greatness of our sin, but we know our salvation is greater. We know we deserve punishment but we believe we shall receive mercy! We have a sure confidence in the mercy and forgiveness of God.

Return to the story of the prodigal son. It was repentance that awakened him to his condition, brought him to conviction, and motivated him to change. But it was faith that gave him the confidence to know that when he returned home, he would be loved and forgiven. He knew mercy would triumph over judgment. If he had not believed that, he would never have dared to go home.

Repentance and faith go hand-in-hand. Repentance breeds awareness; belief fosters confidence. And our belief is rooted in the nature of God. We believe *God is love.* So we also believe he is more willing to heal us than hurt us—to receive us than to turn us away. In the words of 1 John 4:18, "perfect love drives out fear." We are not afraid to go home!

---

[10]Jackson, *Works,* 5:380 (sermon: "Sermon on the Mount —IX").

Wesley preached the love of God because he was convinced that when anyone was gripped by this love, he would want to go home. Sadly, there are still many who do not have this concept of God. And having a basically negative concept, they are not moved to establish a relationship with him. But if we can accept a God who is *love*—love by nature and love by choice—then we can love a God like that!

The second element in belief is assurance. More will be said about this in the next chapter, but it is important to see the relationship between saving faith and assurance. Saving faith brings a note of certainty into our lives. Through faith we know that Jesus is truly the Son of God. We see Jesus as the only foundation of salvation.[11] It is interesting to note how the theme of assurance runs through Wesley's record of his experience at Aldersgate:

> I felt my heart strangely warmed. I felt
> I did trust in Christ, Christ alone for sal-
> vation: And an assurance was given me
> that he had taken away my sin, even mine,
> and saved me from the law of sin and
> death.[12]

Wesley saw reliance as the third element in belief. In the act of faith we switch the control center of our lives from ourselves to Christ. In the past we relied on our power and intellect, now we rely on Christ. The early church described this reliance in the affirmation, "Jesus is Lord." By that they meant initially a reliance on Christ to save them from their sins. Wesley likewise saw the Cross as the focal point

----

[11]Jackson, *Works*, 5:137 (sermon: "The Witness of Our Own Spirit").

[12]Ibid., 1:103 (Journal, May 24, 1738).

of our deliverance. He wrote, "Nothing in the Christian system is of greater consequence than the doctrine of the Atonement."[13]

But to affirm Christ's lordship also means that we look to him for life in the present. We serve a risen Savior. We acknowledge him to be our sovereign, provider, and empowerer. Here is where the dynamic of Wesleyan discipleship is seen. Through saving faith we appropriate the power of Christ to every dimension of our lives. He forgives the past, heals the present, and offers hope for the future. Consequently, reliance never ceases. In this way we can affirm with the saints of the ages, "I have been saved, I am being saved, and I shall be saved."

For Wesley, belief was ultimately expressed in obedience. The test of "knowing Christ" is whether or not we obey him. We do not go far in our Christian walk before we discover the troublesomeness of this truth. We quickly learn that it is one thing to profess faith but it is something else to express it. Wesley drove this point home whenever he could. And he understood obedience in the broadest of terms. He desribed it as "obedience to all the commands of God, internal and external; obedience of the heart and of the life: in every temper and all manner of life."[14] Such obedience was not based on a cold sense of duty, but rather on an intense hunger to do God's will. Obedience is joyful, not legalistic. This does not mean that every experience will be easy, comfortable, or enjoyable. Some things are done "against the grain" and only by sheer force of the

---

[13]Telford, *Letters*, 6:297–98.
[14]Jackson, *Works*, 5:220 (sermon: "The Marks of the New Birth").

will. But it does mean that obedience to Christ (easy or difficult) will bring a sense of fulfillment to our lives.

This is the Wesleyan description of saving faith. It begins in repentance and climaxes in belief. In repentance we turn from a life without Chirst; in belief we complete the turn by moving to embrace Christ's way as our way. And in that process, salvation is begun. Beyond the initial commitment there will be a lifetime of development and progress.

I hope this view of faith is inviting to you. It is a view that makes Christianity dynamic and not static. Too often we give the impression that our salvation is *completed* in a single, dramatic experience. We hear endless testimonies of people who were saved "x" years ago. While Wesley would rejoice in this, he would go on to ask, "But are you saved today, in this moment?" He would want to know if the experience of the past was still alive in the present.

Wesley had an interesting picture of salvation. He compared it to a house. He called repentance the porch of religion. Justification was the door. All the rooms in the house were facets of our sanctification. By using this analogy he was trying to tell us that after the experience of conversion, there is a whole house (lifetime) to be explored.[15] There are effects of salvation, continuing dimensions and implications of our conversion. We must continue to walk and grow. Otherwise we will remain in the hallways of the total experience God has for us.

We are now standing at the door. In the chapters that follow, we must walk through and into some of

---

[15]Jackson, *Works*, 8:472. Cf. Telford, *Letters*, 2:268.

the rooms. But perhaps here is a good place to stand for a moment, giving thanks to God for saving faith and committing ourselves to the lifelong quest of exploring all the rooms of our spiritual house.

For Discussion

1. The author describes salvation from two sides: divine and human. Is this a new way to look at it for you? If so, how do you respond to this perspective?

2. Which element in repentance strikes you as being most important? Why?

3. Which element in belief strikes you as being most important? Why?

4. How does your testimony reflect the truth that salvation is dynamic (ongoing), not static (completed in a single, past action)?

For Further Reading

Sermon, "Salvation By Faith" Works, 5:7–16.

Sermon, "Scriptural Christianity" Works, 5:37–52.

Sermon, "Justification By Faith" Works, 5:53–64.

Sermon, "The Righteousness of Faith" Works, 5:65–75.

Sermon, "The Way to the Kingdom" Works, 5:76–86.

Sermon, "Marks of the New Birth" Works, 5:212–22.

Sermon, "Sermon on the Mount—IX" Works, 5:378–92.

Transformation (Effects of Salvation)

In his conception of salvation Wesley combines a sense of complete dependence on God with a sense of man's complete responsibility.

Burtner & Chiles

5
Transformation
(Effects of Salvation)

I can still remember the first time I visited an electric power plant. Even though I was only a child, no one had to tell me I was in the presence of power. Just being there was enough to know it. Conversion is like that. Even though it has never happened to you before, you know you're in the presence of power. It is not a vague imperceptible experience. It is an experience of power.

Christians believe there are some discernable effects of conversion. In this chapter we will examine some of them. It is important to remember that we are not looking at separate experiences. What we will examine is all part of one experience. Wesley taught that there are several effects in the one experience of conversion. Keeping the picture of a rope in mind may help. A rope is a single thing, but it is made up of many strands. Likewise, in conversion, several things happen to us.

First of all, Wesley taught that we are *justified*. In teaching this he was one with the Protestant Reformers and the saints of the ages. He recognized that justification by faith was the heart of the gospel. By justification he meant what God does *for* us. Wesley saw that sin had rendered people incapable of saving themselves. The only option left was the intervention of God. When God intervened to justify us, he did two important things. First, he pardoned us for the sins of the past. Wesley wrote, "The plain scriptural notion of justification is pardon, the forgiveness of sins."[1]

Wesley ministered before the age of modern psychology, but he knew the liberating power of forgiveness. And he saw the totality of forgiveness. He spoke of the pardoned sinner and said, "His sins, all his past sins, in thought, word, and deed, are covered, are blotted out, shall not be remembered or mentioned against him, any more than if they had not been."[2] It is not surprising that people responded to Wesley's message, for he was addressing the problem of unresolved guilt. Many of his hearers felt the guilt, but did not know how to resolve it. Wesley made it clear that in Christ forgiveness is already a reality.

In my ministry I have run up against a practical problem in this regard. I have counseled those who said, "I guess I'm not forgiven because I can't forget it." Somewhere along the line they have gotten the idea that God's forgiveness and their ability to forget go hand in hand. But notice, God speaks through his Word and says, "*I* will remember your sins no more" (Isa. 43:25). He does not say, "You will remember your sins no more." Only God can forgive *and* forget. Some things we've done will be in our memories as long as we live. The message of the

---

[1]Jackson, *Works*, 5:57 (sermon: "Justification by faith").
[2]Ibid.

gospel is not the erasure of memory, but rather the healing of our memories. Through justification we have memory without condemnation. We are forgiven!

At the same time, we experience a second effect: new birth. This is what God does in us. Wesley called it God's activity of "renewing our fallen nature."[3] He used the analogy of physical birth to describe the process. In physical birth something comes into existence that has never been alive before. In conversion our spiritual nature comes alive in a way it has never been before.

For one thing, there is a renewal of the image of God. In the chapter dealing with original sin we saw that the Fall corrupted the image of God by radically weakening the natural image and destroying the moral image. But Wesley saw new birth as the renewal of righteousness and true holiness—the renewal of the moral image. He called it "that great change which God works in the soul when he brings it into life; when he raises it from the death of sin to the life of righteousness."[4] By this act we are made new creatures in Christ and restored to the full humanity God intended for us before the Fall.

In physical birth there is passage from fetal to full existence. Such a passage is essential if there is to be mature life. We are meant to live outside the womb. In the new birth there is also passage. We pass from spiritual death to spiritual life. We are made to live beyond the confines of sin. Related to this is the idea of power. When we are born, we are

---

[3]Jackson, *Works*, 6:71 (sermon: "The New Birth").
[4]Ibid.

empowered to accomplish certain things. Likewise, new birth empowers us to live above sin. These notions of the Christian's relationship to sin are some of the strongest points in Wesley's theology. He firmly believed that a Christian was enabled to overcome sin.

Unfortunately, Wesley has been misunderstood at this point. Some have interpreted him to mean the actual eradication of sin. By this they have given the impression that Wesley believed the possibility of sin is removed. It is best to let Wesley speak for himself. In the sermon "The Scripture Way of Salvation" he spoke to this issue by saying,

> Hence may appear the extreme mischievousness of that seemingly innocent opinion that there is no sin in a believer, that all sin is destroyed, root and branch, the moment a man is justified. By totally preventing that repentance which follows justification, it quite blocks up the way to sanctification. There is no place for repentance in him who believes there is no sin either in his heart or life. Consequently, there is no place for his being perfected in love, to which that repentance is indispensably necessary.[5]

Wesley makes it clear that sin remains in the one who is justified, but it does not have to reign.[6] The error in the idea of eradication is that it treats sin as a "thing." We have already seen that for Wesley, sin is

---

[5]Jackson, Works, 6:51 (sermon: "The Scripture Way of Salvation"). The words, "which follow justification" are added to interpret which repentance Wesley had in mind.

[6]Ibid., p. 50.

relational not substantial. Since it is not a "thing," it cannot be excised like a surgeon removes a tumor. A better word than removal is reconciliation, which is a relational word. Reconciliation speaks of a process of restoring a relationship that has been estranged. For Wesley, that is what new birth does. It rebuilds the bridge between God and man. It reopens the lines of communication. It reactivates the relationship that sin has deadened. And when it is restored, there is no reason that it ever has to be destroyed again.

In saying that Wesley taught victory over sin, it is necessary to understand what he meant by "sin." He tells us himself: "By sin, I have understood outward sin . . . an actual, voluntary transgression of the law, acknowledged to be such at the time it is transgressed."[7] It is *very* important to remember this. Wesley always left open the possibility of involuntary sin, but he did not feel this sin would bring God's condemnation. And on the other side of the coin, he believed that a person was so empowered at justification that he could, in every case, choose the way of righteousness. No Christian *has* to sin; no Christian is *inevitably* bound to sin. Wesley had examples of individuals who sinned after they were "born of God."[8] His conclusion was that if a person did not continue to keep watch over his life, he could lapse into sin after justification. But he also wanted to stress that sin after conversion is not a necessity.

With this in mind it is possible to see more clearly what Wesley meant by overcoming sin. He meant that in conversion God gives grace powerful

---

[7]Jackson, *Works*, 5:227 (sermon: "The Great Privilege of Those Born of God").

[8]Ibid., pp. 227–32.

enough to forgive us of all our *past* sins and powerful enough to fortify our wills against any future situation that might lead us to sin. Wesley could conceive of no moment or event more powerful than the grace of God. Grace is always greater than sin. Any return to sin is a problem of the will, not a problem of grace. The new birth renews the image of God, and that renewal powerfully keeps us and moves us toward full maturity in Christ.

Consequently, Wesley could speak of the third strand: initial sanctification. Justification is what God does *for* us. New birth is what God does *in* us. Initial sanctification is what God *begins* in us. Wesley said that in conversion, inward and outward holiness begins.[9] And in this beginning several important things happen, which enable us to mature in the Christian life.

First, real righteousness begins. For Wesley it was unthinkable that God would call a person something he was not.[10] In conversion God not only declares us righteous, he actually makes us righteous with the righteousness of Christ. It is not a perfected righteousness that needs no further development, but it is genuine righteousness.

This is consistent with our view of sin as disease. When medicine is given to us, we are made healthy with the healing power it brings. The doctor doesn't simply declare us to be well, he gives us something that works a real change in our bodies. We are made healthy with the health-giving properties of the medicine. The result is genuine healing. In

---

[9]Jackson, *Works*, 6:71–72 (sermon: "The New Birth").
[10]Ibid., 10:203; 271–83.

the spiritual life this means that when God says, "You are righteous," he does not do it with no basis in fact or with his fingers crossed. Rather, we are infused with the righteousness of Christ, which genuinely transforms our character.

Related to this is an authentic purity. In conversion our hearts are cleansed from sin and made fit dwelling places for the Spirit. The activity of the Spirit from within works to transform our total life. Personal holiness expands into social holiness. Salvation from sin becomes salvation for service. What God has done in our spirits, he now moves out to do in our bodies, minds, emotions, and relationships.

It is important to see that Wesley is speaking about *initial* sanctification. He never intended that we should rest in or rely on a single spiritual experience. By terming it "initial sanctification" he was attempting to keep the dynamism of grace and point to the need for future growth in grace, knowledge, and righteousness. It is not inappropriate to say that Wesley's theology can always be summarized in the exhortation to "Go on!"

Lane Adams has written a book entitled *How Come It's Taking Me So Long to Get Better?* The title alone is intriguing, but he uses an illustration that comes close to capturing what Wesley meant. Adams writes that during World War II the American forces used a "beach-head strategy" to capture islands in the South Pacific. Their goal was to capture a piece of the island, no matter how small. Then from the beach-head they worked their way out until they could claim the entire island.

Wesley is saying something similar. At the moment of conversion, the Holy Spirit captures a portion of our lives for God. The extent of that initial capture varies with each person, and no one would claim (in looking back) that God got it all the first time. But He did get a place to call His own. And from that dimension of our lives, the Spirit began to move out until more and more of our lives are under His control. This is the Wesleyan dynamic of grace that recognizes genuine change, while at the same time acknowledging the need for continued growth.

These then are the major effects of salvation. Justification gives us a new standing before God. New birth gives us a new power to deal with sin and live for Christ. And initial sanctification begins the authentic development of Christlike character and provides a base for the Holy Spirit to purify and empower our lives.

In this regard it is helpful for me to keep the idea of a football game in mind. Every week millions of fans pack stadiums to watch their favorite teams compete. But what do you suppose would happen if people took their seats and then heard something like this over the loudspeaker: "Today we are arbitrarily beginning this game in the middle of the second quarter and supposing that the score is twenty one to fourteen in favor of the home team." People would look at each other in dismay. They would be confused and bewildered. They know you do not play football that way. They would ask, "What happened to the kickoff?" There has to be a kickoff.

Jesus said, "You must be born again." You cannot leave it out. You cannot move on to other things. But at the same time you do not have kickoffs and then go home. There are four full quarters to play for the game to be complete. The kickoff begins it all and sets the stage for the rest. Conversion begins it all. It brings to our lives those dynamics that enable us to live the rest of our lives for Christ. These effects are meant to lead us into the future and equip us for effective discipleship. Through conversion the Spirit of God is in us, not only to deal with the past, but also to give us a vision for the future. And as far as living is concerned, that is the best effect of salvation!

For Discussion

1. In what ways does Wesley's theology help you avoid the problem of looking back to a single conversion experience as the sum total of Christian experience?

2. How do you respond to Wesley's belief that God never calls a person something he is not?

3. Consider each term—*justification, new birth,* and *initial sanctification.* What importance does each have in your Christian experience?

For Further Reading

Sermon, "Salvation By Faith" *Works,* 5:7–16.

Sermon, "The Scripture Way of Salvation" *Works,* 6:43–54.

Sermon, "Justification By Faith" *Works,* 5:53–64.

Sermon, "The First Fruits of the Spirit" *Works,* 5:87–97.

Sermon, "The New Birth" *Works,* 5:65–76

Sermon, "The Marks of the New Birth" Works, 5:212–22.

Sermon, "The Great Privilege of Them That Be Born of God" Works, 5:223–33.

Sermon, "The Wilderness State" Works, 6:77–90.

Sermon, "On Sin In Believers" Works, 6:144–55.

Don't Stop Now
(Growth in Grace)

What one believes about human nature and God's grace will have a direct bearing on the kind of Christian life one experiences.

Mildred Wynkoop

6
Don't Stop Now
(Growth in Grace)

Wesley's theology is a theology of grace. No matter where we are in our spiritual life, we got there by grace and we can go on in grace. The call of the Christian is the call to grow. The Wesleyan equation is this: "Grace plus response equals growth." There is no point in life where we can say, "I have all I need."

But how do we grow? Wesley believed that God has provided certain experiences and means by which we may grow in grace. One of the major emphases in his ministry was to nurture people in their faith. Unfortunately, this dimension of his ministry has often been overshadowed by his role as a traveling evangelist. While it is true that Wesley traveled far and wide to win people to Christ, it is equally true that, having won them, he sought to make disciples of them. He wanted more than bare converts or spiritual infants. He wanted people who were able to live the Christian life day by day and who could in turn bring others to faith. Therefore, he emphasized elements that contribute to growth in grace.

First, he taught that we grow in grace out of a

sense of assurance. An assured faith is one of the
central themes in Wesleyan theology. Wesley's favorite text in this regard was Romans 8:16, "The
Spirit himself testifies with our spirit that we are
God's children." In the early days of his ministry he
felt so strongly about assurance that he taught there
was no authentic salvation without it. By the mid
1740s he had modified his position saying that while
assurance was not *necessary* for salvation it was the
"common privilege of all believers."[1]

Here as at other times Wesley let experience be
his teacher. In his ministry he had found those persons who could testify to a salvation experience but
who were still plagued by doubts and questions. He
came to see this as one of the tools of Satan to rob the
new believer of joy, peace, and power. Consequently,
he preached the doctrine of assurance all the more,
but now for motivation to grow rather than as a condition for salvation.

We can understand this if we return to Wesley's
understanding of Christianity as a relationship. Authentic growth takes place when there is security
and love in a relationship. Wesley said this is what
the Holy Spirit provides. He comes to our hearts to
let us know that we are God's children. We do not
have to live with a "hope-so, think-so, maybe-so"
faith. Dr. Ed Robb has said that if salvation is so
insignificant that you can have it and not know it,
then you can lose it and not tell it. It is the ministry
of the Holy Spirit to bear witness to us that we *are*
the children of God.

---

[1]Telford, *Letters*, 2:91. Robert Tuttle's book, *John Wesley:
His Life and Theology* (Grand Rapids: Zondervan, 1979) has a
helpful discussion of Wesley's views on assurance, pp. 199–211.

Unfortunately, assurance has been misunderstood. Some see it as impossible. They maintain it is not part of what God chooses to give his children. The best we can do is live with a rather high degree of tentativeness. For such people, to speak of assurance undercuts any motivation to growth. But we have shown (and will demonstrate further) that Wesley himself preached assurance as a motivation to growth. Assurance was not Methodism's "eternal security." For Wesley, assurance dealt with one's *present* relationship, it was no guarantee for the future. Only continued obedience and faithfulness could take care of the future.

Still others have seen any testimony of assurance as an expression of pride. They say, "To speak of an assured faith sounds like spiritual conceit." To be sure, if one testifies to assurance based on any special experience or performance, it is conceit. For Wesley, true assurance is *not* saying, "Look what a great Christian I am." Rather it is saying, "Look what a great Savior I have!" Here is the point of assurance: Christ has powerfully entered our lives, and it is His intention to stay.

Despite misunderstandings, a legitimate question remains. Is there anything on which to base assurance? Can we distinguish between true assurance and presumption? Is there a way to be sure we are not fooling ourselves? Wesley would answer yes to these questions. He provided a series of tests which a person could use to judge the authenticity of his assurance.[2]

---

[2]Jackson, *Works*, 5:117–23 (sermon: "The Witness of the Spirit").

First, he taught as Paul said, that there is the witness of the Spirit. The Holy Spirit will not call us something we are not. Wesley wrote, "We must be holy of heart and holy in life before we can be conscious that we are so."[3] The first movement is God's. We love him because he *first* loved us (1 John 4:10). Wesley wanted it to be clearly understood that assurance has an objective base. We do not dream it up. It is a gift from God, mediated to us through the Holy Spirit and on the basis of Christ's atonement.[4] When the Spirit bears witness, he does so to something that has actually occurred.

Second, there is the test of the witness of our own spirit. When we examine ourselves, we can be aware of at least four elements that confirm God's grace in our lives. First, we know that we have repented of our sins. In the last chapter we showed that repentance does not happen apart from the exercise of our wills. It is a conscious determination to change. Therefore, Wesley said, we can know that we have repented. Second, we are aware of a change in our lives. Wesley called it a change from darkness to light, from the power of Satan to the power of God.[5] Third, we are aware of a new character produced in us. Here is where the fruit of the Spirit comes in. (Gal. 5:22–23) And fourth, we find joy in the service of God. Wesley said, "A true lover of God hastens to do His will on earth as it is done in heaven."[6]

Through these tests, Wesley believed any person

---

[3]Jackson, *Works*, p. 115.
[4]Ibid.
[5]Ibid., pp. 118–9.
[6]Ibid., p. 120.

could distinguish between true assurance and presumption. Having come to the conclusion that assurance is well founded, he believed we would be joyously motivated to grow in the grace and knowledge of Jesus Christ.

Wesley's second major teaching on growth in grace had to do with the practical ways in which such growth takes place. For him, it occurred through the use of the means of grace. The "means of grace" was a particular term in Protestant and Roman Catholic circles to describe the specific channels through which God conveys grace to his people. Wesley never limited God's grace to these "means," he only believed that the means of grace were the normal (ordinary) ways that God enabled the believer to grow in grace.[7]

Before discussing the various means of grace, a general statement is in order. Wesley did not believe the means of grace had any power in themselves. Use of them alone did not guarantee growth in grace. The means of grace were just that: means, not ends in themselves. Therefore, when he advocated the use of the means of grace it was never in a legalistic or mechanistic sense. But he did believe that these usual channels were used by God to communicate his grace to people. He divided the means of grace into two groups: the instituted means (those ordained by Christ), and the prudential means (those ordained by the Church). The instituted means were his primary focus, but he also felt God has chosen to work through the prudential means as well.

The first instituted means of grace is *prayer.*

---

[7]Jackson, *Works,* p. 187 (sermon: "The Means of Grace").

This came first in Wesley's list because of his under-standing of Christianity as a relationship. He called prayer "the grand means of drawing near to God" and felt that all the other means should be mixed with prayer.[8] At the heart was Wesley's knowledge that all relationships—human and divine—require good communication. He recognized prayer as the means of that communication between God and man.

In one of my own revival meetings a man came confessing spiritual dryness. Upon inquiring about his relationship with God, I discovered he had not prayed with regularity or meaning for over a year. As we talked further, I continued to sense that this was the heart of his problem. The lines of communication were down; consequently he was not receiving any fresh word from God or feeling that his words were reaching their intended destination.

Wesley called the lack of prayer the common cause of "the wilderness state" (a sense of spiritual dryness and purposelessness). He went on to say that the lack of prayer in one's life cannot be made up for by any other means.[9] Believing in the indispensible nature of prayer as he did, Wesley urged his people to be faithful in private and public prayer. His own life was a model of discipline and regularity in prayer. The hours of every day were undergirded and saturated with prayer. As a result, he experi-enced growth in grace.

The second instituted means of grace is what Wesley called, "searching the Scriptures." He knew

---

[8]Telford, *Letters,* 4:90.
[9]Jackson, *Works,* 6:81 (sermon: "The Wilderness State").

the power of the Bible. He referred to himself as a man of one book, and he wanted the Methodists to be Bible Christians.[10] To aid his followers in the use of Scripture, he compiled explanatory notes for both the Old and New Testaments and made them available at reasonable prices.[11] Wesley's emphasis upon the primacy of Scripture was based on the conviction that through the Bible God gives, confirms, and increases true wisdom.

Accordingly, he laid down certain principles that would increase one's knowledge of the Word and allow it to have its greatest effect. First, he wanted a person to know the whole Bible, not just parts of it. He advocated reading from both Testaments each day. Second, he did believe that a regular reading of the Bible was most profitable for spiritual growth. His own practice was usually to follow the suggested readings in the table of lessons in the Book of Common Prayer. However, he maintained an inner freedom to read wherever he felt God was directing him. Third, he believed that one should carefully apply and immediately put into practice what was read. He had little use for a detached reading of Scripture. Instead, he wanted readers to ask, "What does this mean for me?" and "How can I put the truth of Scripture to work for the good of others?" In this way, the Bible served as an important means of grace.

---

[10]See Telford, *Letters*, 4:299; Jackson, *Works*, vol. 11; Jackson, *Works*, 8:339–47 for Wesley's view concerning his own life and the lives of early Methodists.

[11]The *Explanatory Notes Upon the New Testament* were published in 1755, and the *Explanatory Notes Upon the Old Testament* followed in 1765.

The Lord's Supper stood third in the instituted means of grace. Wesley averaged communing once every four or five days. He exhorted early Methodists to practice "constant communion," which included being present whenever possible at the Holy Communion. On many occasions he personally led Methodists from their preaching houses to the Anglican parish churches in order that they might receive the sacrament. When Anglicans no longer welcomed Methodists at their altars, he found other legitimate ways of providing the Lord's Supper for his followers.

Why was he so concerned that the Methodists receive the sacrament at every opportunity? Because he believed the experience was more than a symbol, it was an opportunity to actually commune with Christ and receive the grace of God. He stopped short of any notion of transubstantiation, but he believed that Christ was present in the service. Normally, the Lord's Supper would be of greatest benefit to believers, an aid to growth in grace. But Wesley also believed the sacrament had a converting potential. Consequently, his invitation was an open one, extended to anyone who truly and earnestly repented of sin, was in love and charity with neighbor, and intended to lead a new life following the commandments of God. This being so, the Lord's Supper became the high point in early Methodist worship.[12]

The fourth instituted means of grace was fasting. In the earlier part of his life and ministry, Wesley observed Wednesdays and Fridays as fast days. This

---

[12]One of the finest treatments of Wesley's view of the Lord's Supper is John Bowmer's *The Sacrament of the Lord's Supper in Early Methodism* (London: Dacre Press, 1951).

was in keeping with the practices of the early Christians. Later on, he dropped Wednesday and exhorted his followers to faithfully keep Friday as a day of fasting. It is important to see that Wesley did not see fasting as an act of mortification, or even as a lengthy experience. He did not believe the effectiveness of fasting lay in its duration or intensity, but rather in the commitment of time exclusively for God and spiritual concerns.

Normally, Wesley began his fast after the evening meal on Thursday evening and broke it with tea on Friday afternoon. In between he gave particular time to prayer and devotion. When the occasion demanded, he was open to longer fasts. But as an ongoing means of grace he felt this regular practice was sufficient. Through these weekly fasts he believed God mediated grace to enrich the Christian life.[13]

The fifth instituted means of grace was group fellowship, or what Wesley called, "Christian conference." As it turned out, this means became the primary instrument of early Methodist renewal. Wherever Wesley preached, he sought to organize believers into bands, classes, and societies for their continuing nurture. In 1743, he organized these groups into the United Societies, a movement within the Church of England. Methodism remained as a "little church" within the larger body until shortly after Wesley's death.

It is interesting to see the various dynamics at work in these three units of Methodist nurture. The bands were groups of four to eight people of the same sex and as near the same maturity in Christ as

[13]Jackson, *Works*, 5:344–60 (sermon: "Upon Our Lord's Sermon on the Mount, Sermon XXVII").

possible. Wesley believed every Christian needed a small, intimate place to share the concerns of his life and to find commonality of experience and intensity of support. The classes were groups of about a dozen, mixed as to sex and levels of experience. In time the classes became the core of Methodist nurture, often being led by lay men and women. The class leader functioned as an "undersheperd" and was responsible for the spiritual and temporal welfare of those in the group. The societies were the largest group in Methodism per se, usually numbering above forty. This group met weekly as well for Bible exposition, singing, testimony, and prayer. When clergymen were available, they gave leadership to the societies, but often these groups were led by the laity as well. On each level, the dynamic was different, but the total experience provided a nearly comprehensive experience of nurture and discipleship.

The importance Wesley placed in this means of grace can be seen in two remarks he made. On one occasion he stated that "preaching like an apostle without joining together those that are awakened and training them up in the ways of God, is only begetting children for the murderer."[14] This was his opinion after a visit to Pembrokeshire where there were no regular societies. His evaluation was that "the consequence is that nine of the ten once-awakened are now faster asleep than ever."[15] He was fully convinced that wherever this dimension of discipleship was lost, Methodism would cease to be a vital movement.

---

[14]Jackson, Works, 3:144.
[15]Ibid.

These then are the five instituted means of grace. Wesley believed God had ordained them as channels through which his converting and confirming grace could flow. In addition to these, Wesley recognized three prudential means of grace: doing no harm, doing all the good you can, and attending the private and public worship of God.[16] He used these means as conditions for continuing membership in the Methodist Societies, and members were regularly examined to see how they were living up to such standards.

At the heart of it was Wesley's conviction that growth in grace is not accidental or automatic. One does not wander or stumble into maturity. On God's side, he does not save us and then tell us to do the best we can. Rather, he supplies specific instruments through which he can nurture us. To be sure, he is not limited to these means, but he has chosen to use them as his primary and normal means of effecting Christian growth. I have yet to meet a vital, growing Christian who did not use these means of grace in one way or another.

There will always be highs and lows, ups and downs, advances and declines. Christians have good days and bad days like everyone else. Not to admit that is to misrepresent the facts. There are mountain-top experiences, but they do not come every day. The key to Christian growth is not feeling but faithfulness. God has expressed his faithfulness by providing means of grace. We express our faithfulness by taking advantage of them. And in that God-human encounter, the connection is made,

---

[16]Jackson, *Works*, 8:323–24.

grace flows into our lives, and we are led to greater conformity to the image of Christ.

For Discussion

1. Consider the equation, "Grace plus response equals growth." What does that mean for your life now?

2. Did the treatment of Wesley's view of assurance shed any new light on the issue for you?

3. Review the various means of grace. Then (1) share a growth experience you have had in relation to one of them, and (2) share any needs you may feel regarding them.

4. Overall, would you say your faith is growing or standing still? How are the means of grace helping, or how might they help as you chart your course for the future?

For Further Reading

Sermon, "The Witness of the Spirit" *Works,* 5:123–33.

Sermon, "The Witness of Our Own Spirit" *Works,* 5:134–43.

Sermon, "The Wilderness State" *Works,* 6:77–90.

Sermon, "The Means of Grace" *Works,* 5:185–201.

Sermon, "Sermon on the Mount—VII" *Works,* 5:344–60.

Sermon, "The Duty of Constant Communion" *Works,* 7:147–57.

"The Nature, Design, and General Rules of the United Societies in London, Bristol, Kingswood, etc." *Works,* 8:269–71.

"Rules of the Band Societies" *Works,* 8:272–74.

The Heart of It All (Christian Perfection)

It is good to know that after the passage of another century, Methodist theologians are once more exploring the important truths underlined in Wesley's teaching on Christian Perfection.

Frank Baker

7

The Heart of It All
(Christian Perfection)

Wesley viewed the doctrine of Christian perfection as the "grand depositum" of Methodism. He believed God had raised up the people called Methodist to proclaim this truth.[1] Unfortunately today, there is no element in Wesley's theology that causes more trouble than this. On one extreme are those who virtually ignore the doctrine. On the other extreme are those who would make Christian perfection the all-important element in Christian experience and the window through which the rest of Wesleyan theology is viewed. In between are the vast majority of mainline Methodists who either have not heard the doctrine, or who have been confused by what they have heard. Either case is unfortunate, for it leaves Wesley's doctrine in a position he never intended.

Before much progress can be made, two things need to be admitted. First, the doctrine of Christian perfection cannot be omitted from any serious examination of Wesley's theology. Nor can it be omitted

---

[1]Telford, *Letters*, 8:238. It is important to note that this was written less than a year before Wesley's death. He held this view throughout his lifetime.

from a contemporary interpretation of Christian experience. Second, Wesley does not answer every question about the doctrine we would like to ask. The result is a kind of tension between items one and two—a tension that can never be fully resolved. We are left to interpret the doctrine as faithfully as we can, knowing that we are in the spirit of Wesley when we do.

The place to begin is with the word "perfection." This more than anything else throws people off the track, and that right at the start. They hear the word and exclaim, "No one can be *perfect!*" Obviously not, if you mean perfection in terms of absolute purity or flawless performance. But Wesley did not use the term perfection in that sense. We miss the point if we read a modern, dictionary definition of perfection and equate it with Wesley's definition. Notice that he modified "perfection" with the significant adjective, "Christian." Immediately, the term is put in a new context. Wesley is advocating *Christian* perfection, and that puts it in a new and attainable light. We will see how this is so as we move along.

But even Christian perfection has its limits. For one thing, it is not spiritual infallibility. Wesley made it plain that the Christian is still liable to sin, and does not possess absolute knowledge, absolute judgment, or absolute performance.[2] Wesley termed such notions "angelism" and felt that to make it appear so high was to effectually renounce it.[3] Wesley constantly maintained that Christian perfection is for real people in this life.

[2]Jackson, Works, 6:2–7 (sermon: "Christian Perfection").
[3]Telford, Letters, 5:20.

Second, Christian perfection does not make one a superior Christian. Wesley rejected any idea of a status system among believers. On the contrary, he felt anyone who experienced Christian perfection would be filled with humility.[4] Such a one would never entertain ideas of being better than anyone else. As with everything else in the Christian faith, the experience of Christian perfection is of *grace*, not of works lest anyone should boast.

Third, Christian perfection is not immunity from life's problems. In fact, the Devil seems to delight in defeating those who are closest to God (1 Peter 5:8). Christians are exposed to the same germs, the same natural laws, and the same temptations as any other person.[5] Christian perfection is not a vaccination against reality.

Fourth, Christian perfection is not a static, one-time experience. To be sure, Wesley identified it with a spiritual "crisis" (significant event) in one's pilgrimage. He taught that a person could be entirely sanctified in an instant.[6] But it is important to note that he never separated the "moment" from one's total Christian experience. When Wesley spoke of the instantaneous nature of Christian perfection he usually stressed the process that precedes and follows it.[7] The event was always kept in balance with the larger activity of God's grace.

No illustration perfectly captures what is going on here, but I have come to see it as analogous to the relationship between a moment of time and time

---

[4]Jackson, *Works*, 11:427.
[5]Ibid., 6:5.
[6]Ibid., 11:446.
[7]Ibid.

itself. Place a clock in front of you. Once a day on
that clock it is precisely "high noon." For a moment
it is exactly twelve o'clock. This moment is real and
necessary. In fact, if you have a camera, you can take a
picture the instant the second hand sweeps across the
twelve. You can capture and describe that moment.
But "high noon" loses its significance when it is divorced from the movement of the second hand before
and after the moment itself. Moments in time are only
meaningful in light of the fact that time moves.

Christian perfection is like that. There is sanctifying grace that may operate in one's life "in a moment." The experience can be noted and described.
But the experience loses its full significance when it is
divorced from the larger activity of grace before and
after. God's grace leads us to the place of Christian
perfection (narrowly viewed), and it leads us on after
the experience itself. That's why Wesley could urge
those who testified to this experience to "go on to
perfection" in the ultimate, heavenly sense.

Having looked at some of the things Christian
perfection is not, we may now move to a considera-
tion of its positive features. It is important not to
misunderstand the experience, but it is more important to explore the actual dynamics of it. Most im-
portantly, it is singleness of intention. The heart of
Christian perfection is in the will, not in one's actions. Actions vary, intentions can remain constant.[8]

---

[8]Wesley borrowed here from the rich tradition of the past,
particularly from the eastern church fathers (e.g., Gregory of
Nyssa), and from persons like Thomas á Kempis, Juliana of Nor-
wich, Françis Fénelon, Jeremy Taylor, and William Law. All of
these (and many others) placed the heart of Christianity in one's
intentions and motives—often calling it "perfect love."

To speak of Christian perfection as singleness of intention does not minimize actions. But it does mean that the experience of being is deeper than the level of doing. It means we have discovered a central purpose for life—a purpose that gives meaning, direction, and power to life. For Wesley, the central purpose was captured in Matthew 22:37–38—"Love the Lord your God with all your heart. . . . Love your neighbor as yourself." Wesley saw (as did many before him) that the primary intention, the controlling desire, is our resolve to love God and others.

But how can this love be called "perfect" by God, while at the same time being flawed? An illustration from parenting can provide a clue. When each of my own children were small, they had the bright idea to bring mommy some flowers. Never mind that they plucked the flowers from the bed mommy had worked hard to cultivate. Never mind that they might have even taken flowers from the neighbor's bed! Their one desire was to please mommy and to show their love for her. So, in they came with flowers, weeds, and dirt. With faces aglow they exclaimed, "Mommy, we love you!"

What did mommy do? Did she throw the flowers away because they had clumps of weeds and grass clinging to them? Did she refuse to accept them because they were pulled from her bed or the bed of a neighbor? Of course not! She saw the deed through the eyes of love, took her nicest vase, and proudly displayed the flowers on the table. She accepted the act of love, even though she might follow it (at an appropriate time) with a lesson in flower picking.

So it is with God. He accepts our intentions. He sees our motives. It has to be this way, for in the light of his impeccable holiness even our best actions fall short. The Bible puts it this way, even our best actions look like filthy rags in comparison to God. We cannot hope to match him in actions, but we can be one with him in motive. Our controlling desire can be to do his will on earth as it is in heaven. God knows whether or not that is our intention, and when it is, he calls it "perfect" even though it comes packaged with some weeds and dirt.

By taking this approach, God does not ignore or minimize sin. Even perfect Christians are convicted when their actions and attitudes are improper.[9] Like a good parent, God has to take us aside, point out our mistakes, and teach us how to bring our lives into greater conformity to his will. But the point is that he does not negate the relationship when performance is flawed. Those of us who are married know that we operate under this system everyday. If we have to relate to each other in marriage, and in fact we want to relate to each other this way, *how much more* is God willing to do the same!

The beautiful irony is that by starting with intentions first, God more powerfully moves us to change than if he started with legalism. Counselors' offices are filled with people who experienced discipline without love and legalism without affection. Such persons struggle with low self-esteem and buried resentment toward parents, friends, and associates who never loved them. But when we know we are loved, believed in, and trusted, we really want to do the best we can.

---

[9]Jackson, *Works*, 5:156–70 (sermon: "The Repentance of Believers").

The implications here are numerous, but for the moment it is important to see the connection between motives and actions. Wesley wrote before the days of modern psychology, but he is amazingly contemporary here. He knew that our actions would be more consistent when our motives are fixed. With Jesus, he affirmed that it is out of the heart where deeds are expressed.

So we begin with the powerful truth that Christian perfection is singleness of intention. But secondly, it is *power over sin.*[10] Simply put, Wesley did not believe there was ever a time when a person *had* to sin. In any conceivable situation the grace of God is always greater than the lure of temptation. Wesley knew that as long as we are in the body, temptations to sin will always be there. But he believed the love of God at work in the heart of a person could exclude actual transgression both inwardly and outwardly. The key was to "abide in Christ"—to dwell in the presence of this powerful God.[11]

Notice that intention is related to this dimension as well as to the previous point. If we have settled the issue of sin by a previous commitment to love God and neighbor, then when actual temptations present themselves, power will be there to overcome. Wesley was a realist in acknowledging that even sanctified Christians can sin.[12] But he attributed any departures as failure of will, not a failure of grace. In Christian perfection there is power to overcome sin.

Third, Wesley taught that Christian perfection is

---

[10]Jackson, *Works,* pp. 223–33 (sermon: "The Great Privilege of Those That are Born of God").

[11]Ibid., p. 232.

[12]Ibid.

radical dependence on Christ.[13] Such dependence is total and continuous. It is the recognition that whatever we are and do is the result of his power at work in us. In Wesley's covenant service this was epitomized in the vine-branch relationship of John 15. Here the idea of connection predominates. So long as we are connected to Christ, there will be life, growth, fruit, power, and joy. The perfecting grace of God binds us more closely to Christ.

Dr. J. T. Seamands has described this deepening dependency by speaking of Christian perfection as the movement of Christ in our lives from resident to president. E. Stanley Jones often spoke of it as our act of "full surrender." Robert Munger has described it in his booklet, *My Heart Christ's Home,* as giving Christ every "room" (dimension) of your life, even the closet where yesterday's sin and guilt are stored. In all these ways Christian writers are impressing upon us the fact that as we allow Christ to be Lord over our lives, we increasingly sense our need of him.

Fourth, Christian perfection is *equipment for ministry.* One of the meanings of sanctification is that we are set apart for the service of God. Wesley recognized that Christian perfection is not only a personal experience, but also a social imperative. He called those who testified to the experience of Christian perfection to "do all the good you can to the bodies and souls of men."[14] He kept in balance personal and social holiness. The call remains for the individual and the church to oppose persons and systems that

---

[13]Jackson, *Works,* 11:395–96.
[14]Ibid., p. 432.

are unholy. The mandate to "liberate the captives" is as much in force as ever, and the sanctifying grace of God makes such ministry possible.

Finally, Christian perfection is *an experience to grow in*. Wesley maintained the experience was "improvable."[15] This has been alluded to earlier but it needs to be emphasized on its own. With motives fixed, the Christian cooperates with the grace of God to close the gap between intention and performance. Not to do this would be to make a sham out of Christian perfection.

Another illustration from life can show how perfection can be developed and improved. When each of our children turned four years of age, they were "perfect" as far as the developmental charts were concerned. They could do everything a four-year-old was supposed to do. In that sense we could say, "We have a perfect four year old." But we never believed that was the end of it. We saw their perfection as a fact, but a fact laid against the larger need to continue the maturing process. In fact, their perfection at four years of age had within it the seeds of its own development.

Transferring this into the spiritual dimension, we can see how Wesley could speak of Christian perfection on the one hand and still exhort others to "go on to perfection." The critical factor in Christian perfection is the fixation of motive, the surrender of self-will. With that nailed down, the "perfect Christian" moves on to work out the implications of this commitment.

These then are some of the major dimensions of

---

[15]Jackson, *Works,* p. 442.

Christian perfection. These concepts caused Wesley to believe that God had raised up the people called Methodist to "spread scriptural holiness across the land."[16] He believed Methodism would remain vital only so long as it proclaimed this truth.[17]

This being so, it is necessary to consider the ongoing significance of Christian perfection. Perhaps as you have read you have thought of relevant associations between Wesley's views and your life. For me, the following points are evidences that this message is still needed in the Christian community.

First, Christian perfection maintains dynamism in Christian experience. Ours is a day when discipleship is being stressed. Wesley's theology is particularly relevant because it calls every believer to be growing. There is no room for relying on yesterday's experience, no matter how significant it was. One is always challenged to "go on to perfection." Nominal Christianity will not produce vigorous disciples. Only the deepest of commitments, continually renewed and expanded, will suffice. That is what Christian perfection calls for.

We do not go far in our walk with Christ before we are tempted to relax our devotion. We can come to believe that our past is sufficient to carry us through. Even in Wesley's day people were looking to their baptism as infants as proof that they were Christian. Wesley cut through such attempts and called people to find "proof" in their present relationship with Christ.[18] Christian perfection coun-

---

[16]Jackson, Works, 8:299.
[17]Ibid., 4:83. Wesley expressed similar sentiments in his letters. See, e.g., Telford, Letters, 4:321; 7:109.
[18]Ibid., 6:73–77 (sermon: "The New Birth").

ters the temptation to spiritual inertia. A vigorous proclamation of this truth could move many out of the doldrums and into the dynamic of daily discipleship. People could sense a new depth of God's grace and a fresh realization of their importance in the kingdom.

Second, the doctrine of Christian perfection helps us face our struggles. I am happy to live in a time when we can share our needs openly in the body of Christ. This freedom and climate of concern has given new expression to koinonia. Wesley's doctrine of Christian perfection creates a theological avenue for this kind of sharing. Because we are accepted by God on the basis of our motives, we need not fear sharing our failures of performance. We can call our actions and attitudes by name. We do not have to rationalize or redefine what we are and what we do.

Unfortunately, some Christians (even some who believe in Christian perfection) have felt that admission of failure was tantamount to loss of the experience. Consequently, damaging emotions have been suppressed. Things like anger have been labeled "righteous indignation." Gossip has been spread in the name of "sharing prayer concerns." I have met Christians who have harbored all sorts of need and guilt, but have never felt the freedom to share for fear of judgment and rejection by their brothers and sisters in Christ. Thank God that a positive interpretation of Christain perfection *invites* the sharing of need. Honest confession becomes a doorway through which God's healing grace can flow.

Third, Christian perfection creates unity in life. We all know the tendency to live in compartments.

We all wear several "hats" and find it difficult to juggle them sometimes. It is not uncommon to hear people express the feeling of being pulled in too many directions. When this becomes our norm for living, energy is dissipated.

What a contrast to think that, while we never can eliminate actions and involvement, we can live for one purpose. We can have a controlling motive to live out all our roles for the glory of God and the service of others. It is difficult to grasp the importance of this until it is laid against contemporary emphases on self. Christian perfection calls for a radical other-orientation—toward God and neighbor. The irony is that it offers a depth of fulfillment that cannot be found through the various movements that focus on self-preoccupation.

Biblically, this is confirmed by a David who can accomplish much because he is a man after God's own heart. Paul can do all things through Christ who strengthens him. Psychologically, it is verified in the knowledge that an integrated personality can do more than one that is fragmented. Even the youth of our day are voicing the truth when they exhort each other to "get it all together." The truth of unitive living is important today and it is affirmed in the Christian faith by the doctrine of Christian perfection.

In the scientific realm, the laser beam illustrates Christian perfection's witness to the power of unitive living. In the beam light is concentrated into a single beam that can penetrate the hardest substances known to man. As the diffused light is brought together into the single beam, tremendous power is generated. Wesley was saying the same thing. He was saying that as more and more of our lives are harmonized around a central purpose, we experience greater and greater power.

Finally, Christian perfection points to a consummation. Life is going somewhere. Our perfection is not absolute in this life, but we believe there will come a day when it will be. We will exchange the perishable for the imperishable. Wesley's doctrine of Christian perfection is not an escape from reality because it is firmly rooted in this life. But neither is it bound to this life. It contains the promise of future glory. We are on the way, and that way ends in God's house!

In short, the doctrine of Christian perfection raises our faith above the idea of religion as another "good cause" in society. All of us, whether Christian or not, are already up to our eyeballs in good causes. If Christianity is only one more to add to the list, then we can justifiably say "No." But if Christianity is fundamentally different, that's another matter. If Christianity dares to speak of *transformation* of life in time and eternity in a way that affects all the "good causes", then that's different! The doctrine of Christian perfection makes that claim.

For Discussion

1. In your reading of the chapter were any misconceptions about Christian perfection cleared up?

2. Which point of relevancy strikes you as being most important in your life, the lives of those you know, and the corporate life of the church?

3. Are there other significant relevancies that came to your mind as you read the chapter?

For Further Reading

"A Plain Account of Christian Perfection," *Works,* 11:366–446.

Sermon, "Christian Perfection" *Works,* 6:1–22.

Sermon, "Scriptural Christianity" *Works,* 5:37–52.

Sermon, "The Repentance of Believers" *Works,* 5:156–70.

Sermon, "The Great Privilege of Those That are Born of God" *Works,* 5:223–33.

The End
of the Journey
(Glorification)

This life is only a training ground for the one that is to come.

Colin W. Williams

8
The End of the Journey
(Glorification)

I f Christianity is to have significance, it must deal with eternal issues. The ultimate question on the lips of people is this: "Is this life all there is, or is there more?" This was true in Wesley's day just as it is in ours. He wrote on one occasion that he wanted to know one thing, the way to heaven.[1] In one sense, his whole theology is an attempt to spell out that way.

Wesley would affirm what Colin Williams has written above. He knew that what we are doing (or not doing) in this life shapes us for the life to come. With Keith Miller he would agree that heaven and hell are not so much rewards and punishments as they are consequences. Transformation is begun in this life. Because of that, important things can be said about the end of the journey, about our glorification.

First of all, the kingdom of God is here, now. We do not have to put the emphasis on some future, climactic event outside the bounds of space and time as we know it. As Christians we affirm and look

[1]Jackson, Works, 5:3.

forward to existence in eternity, but we *live* in the present. In fact, I believe it can be said that Christians know how to live fully in the present because they have come to terms with eternity. We have come to see that the kingdom of God is in our midst right now. Wesley called the kingdom, "heaven opened in the soul."[2] And he believed that occurred in this life.

But we do not believe we have experienced everything the kingdom has to offer us. There is a difference between "what is" and "what is to come." So added to our ability to live confidently in the present is the ability to live hopefully with respect to the future. We do not dwell on "the sweet by and by" but we do look forward to the day when our commitment to Christ will not be encumbered by our sinfulness or the limitations of our humanity. We agree with St. Paul that there is coming a time when we will no longer see through a glass darkly, but rather face to face.

But in the meantime we live fully in the present. In fact, Wesley spoke to this very thing when he said, "Your life is continued to you upon the earth for no other purpose than this, that you may know, love, and serve God on earth, and enjoy him to all eternity."[3] Wesley knew that we continually live with one foot in the "now" and the other foot in the "not yet." The kingdom is both present and future, but we are not pulled apart.

Second, the kingdom comes as an active presence. It is not neutral. The Cross is ultimate proof of this truth. Wesley put it this way,

---

[2]Jackson, *Works*, p. 81.
[3]Ibid., 7:230 (sermon: "What Is Man?").

> The substance of all is, "Jesus Christ
> came into the world to save sinners"; or
> "God so loved the world, that he gave his
> only-begotten Son, to the end that we
> might not perish, but have everlasting
> life"; or "He was bruised for our trans-
> gressions, he was wounded for our in-
> iquities, the chastisement of our peace
> was upon him; and with his stripes we are
> healed." Believe this and the Kingdom is
> thine.[4]

Because the kingdom has to be reckoned with as
a presently active reality, we must come to terms one
way or the other with it. The kingdom breaks
through to call us to a decision of acceptance or rejection. Neutrality is not an option. In a sense, God
has forced the issue by coming among us in Jesus
Christ. All the rest of life is a response to that fact and
the implications of it.

This means that the issue of our ultimate glorification is based upon the responses we make to the
presence of the kingdom. It is the activity of the
kingdom that makes a real connection between time
and eternity. Like the ripple effect produced when a
rock falls into the water, the decisions we make
today carry over into our tomorrows. Life is not dis-
jointed. Heaven and earth are connected by the way
we live with regard to kingdom principles.

Third, not everyone is going to respond posi-
tively to the gospel message. Wesley knew that even
though the kingdom was present and active, some
people would decline the offer to live in it. He spoke
of those "who, in spite of all the warnings of God,

---

[4]Jackson, *Works*, 5:85 (sermon: "The Way to the Kingdom").

resolve to have their portion with the devil and his angels.''[5] This meant the loss of authentic existence here and now, but at the moment of death it meant an eternal loss.

On one occasion I had the opportunity to be part of a local church's study of the book of Revelation. A guest minister was invited to bring the overview presentation for the study. Near the end of his address he said, "One of the reasons I am a United Methodist is because John Wesley was a universalist—he believed everyone was going to be saved."

Let there be no misunderstanding; let it be said emphatically that nothing could be farther from the truth. It is true that Wesley believed salvation was offered to everyone. He did believe everyone *could* be saved. But he never believed that all people would be saved. He knew that some people would always prefer darkness to light. Wesley derived no pleasure in proclaiming the reality of eternal death, but he held to the truth as he believed it to be set forth in Scripture. His own words are indicative of that,

> Knowest thou not that the wages of sin is death?—death, not only temporal, but eternal. . . . This is the sentence, to be punished with never-ending death, with everlasting destruction from the presence of the Lord, and from the glory of his power.[6]

As he deemed it appropriate, Wesley urged people to give up the notion that they could remain

---

[5]Jackson, *Works*, 6:382 (sermon: "Of Hell").
[6]Ibid., 5:83.

in their sin and still go to heaven. He told them to be done with any ideas that they could make personal atonement for their sins and thereby "deserve" heaven. He was realistic enough to know that the presence of the kingdom demands a verdict, because it passes judgment on the sinfulness of humanity. This "dark side" of the kingdom message shows that the call to salvation is neither nonsense nor sentimentality. The reality of eternal separation from the presence of God makes the gospel more sobering, real, and urgent. This reality was one of the factors that moved Wesley to do everything humanly possible to win men and women to Christ.

Fourth, the positive aspects of kingdom living outweigh the negative dimensions. While Wesley fully accepted the New Testament doctrine of hell, he emphasized the grace and love of God. He believed this was a more powerful motivation to commitment than fear or threat of punishment. Consequently, he went about preaching the glad tidings of salvation, offering people Christ as Savior from sin and giver of life! In the conference minutes of 1746 he included a statement about overemphasizing the wrath of God. He said that such preaching "generally hardens them that believe not, and discourages them that do."[7] So he preferred to call people to Christ on the basis of love.

At first glance this seems to fit right in with our contemporary emphasis on love. Even in the church there is the emphasis on being loving and affirming. But the contemporary interpretation of love and

---

[7]Albert Outler, *John Wesley* (New York: Oxford Press, 1964), p. 163.

Wesley's understanding part company at one point: accountability. The all-embracing notions of love today include little or no accountability and they make no calls for change. This makes a call to repentance and confession of sin seem antiquated and narrow minded. People say, "If you really loved us, you would not judge us." Wesley would respond, "It is precisely because I do love you that I call you to repent of your sins and align yourself with the will and way of God." The Wesley way is the way of love, and we must be forever glad about that. But it is a love that confronts sin and calls for change. God's love accepts us as we are, but it does not leave us as we are.

Every day as a parent I love my children. I love them to the depths of my soul. But sometimes that love calls them into accountability. Sometimes my love calls for change. There are times when my love is not all-accepting, for to do so would be to affirm unacceptable behavior. So parental love seeks to operate in such a way that my children will grow to be responsible adults. Uncritical, "blind" love would end up producing irresponsibility. Wesley serves us well at the point of making love preeminent, but not to the extent that it overlooks sin and ends up condoning the very things which will destroy what it means to be human.

Given the ideas that have already been shared, Wesley could turn his eye toward heaven and look to a glorious consummation in Christ. He believed God will give,

> an unmixed state of holiness and happiness, far superior to that which Adam enjoyed in Paradise. . . . "God shall wipe

away all tears from their eyes; and there
shall be no more death, neither sorrow nor
crying; Neither shall there be any more
pain; for the former things are done
away!" As there will be no more death
and no more pain or sickness preparatory
thereto; as there will be no more grieving
for, or parting with, friends; so there will
be no more sorrow or crying. Nay, but
there will be a greater deliverance than all
this; for there will be no more sin. And, to
crown all, there will be a deep, intimate,
uninterrupted union with God; a constant
communion with the Father and his Son
Jesus Christ, through the Spirit; a continual enjoyment of the Three-One God,
and of all the creatures in him![8]

Here is one of the strengths of Wesley's theology. It has a word for eternity, but it is a word that
does not divide it from time. The word for the end of
the journey (and beyond) is only a climax to the
word for the start of the journey and its progress. The
life we live now we live by faith in Jesus Christ, and
that alone paves the way for the unspeakable joys of
heaven.

Perhaps the greatest test of anyone's theology is
its ability to sustain him or her in the hour of death.
In his earlier days Wesley had been plagued by the
fear of death. At critical times in his life it had risen
up to render him useless. But as he grew in his
understanding of glorification and its relation to life
here and now, he matured in this area. By holding
together the connectedness of time and eternity,

---

[8]Jackson, *Works*, 6:295–96. (sermon: "The New Creation").

Wesley was able to end his life with words that describe the Christian relationship to time and eternity. Just before he experienced glorification in its ultimate sense, he uttered these simple words, "Best of all is, God is with us."

For Discussion

1. In what ways (verbally and nonverbally) do you see people struggling with the question of eternal life?

2. How does an awareness of our purpose here on earth help settle the question of eternal life?

3. Do you agree that the motive of love is a stronger incentive to commitment than fear? Why?

4. How can the church recover a message of love that still calls for accountability and change? Why do so many see love and accountability as opposites?

For Further Reading

Sermon, "The Great Assize" *Works,* 5:171–84.

Sermon, "Sermon on the Mount: Discourse VII" *Works,* 5:344–60.

Sermon, "Sermon on the Mount: Discourse XI" *Works,* 5:405–12.

Sermon, "On Eternity" *Works,* 6:189–98.

Sermon, "Of Hell" *Works,* 6:381–91.

Sermon, "On the Resurrection of the Dead" *Works,* 7:474–84.

All Together Now
(The Church)

Wesley understood that the concept of the church was at stake in his reforming mission.

Howard Snyder

9

All Together Now
(The Church)

S trictly speaking we have completed our examination of Wesley's "order of salvation." But we
have not fully described his theology. If we stopped
here, we would miss one of his most important
emphases, the church. Wesley was first, last, and always a *churchman* in the finest sense of the term. He
lived and died a clergyman in the Church of England
He believed that authentic Christian experience had
to be nurtured in community. He cared little for
solitary religion. In the next two chapters we must
examine his views as they relate to the church. In
this chapter we shall look at Wesley's theology of the
church. In the next chapter we will consider his
views in relation to church renewal.

In a time when mainline denominations are
floundering and superchurch ecumenism is suspect,
it is not easy to promote a doctrine of the church. All
over the country I meet those who see the church
more as a hindrance than a help. Quaker scholar
Elton Trueblood has described the mood by saying,
"The hardest problem of Christianity is the problem
of the church. We cannot live with it, and we cannot

live without it."[1] The result is a rise in parachurch organizations, which have become substitute churches for many. Programs like "Here's Life America" and polls by George Gallop have confirmed that more people profess a "born-again" experience than can be found actively participating in the churches of our land.

Conditions like this are not as far removed from Wesley as we might first think. In the early eighteenth century institutional religion was largely in eclipse. Spirituality was often promoted by independent and separatist groups. A personally assured faith was often labeled as enthusiasm. When the Evangelical Revival began, Wesley could easily have formed his followers into another denomination, but he didn't. Instead, he remained consciously in the Church of England and sought to revive it from within.[2] When the Methodists were accused of promoting schism in the Anglican Chruch, Wesley replied that he and his followers held "communion therewith in the same manner as they did twenty years ago, and hope to do so until the end of their lives."[3]

All this is to show that a doctrine of the church was important to John Wesley. But the question arises, "What is the church?" In Wesley's own day various answers were given. Some equated it with

---

[1]Frank Bateman Stanger, "Christ is Building His Church," *The Herald*, vol. 94, no. 1 (Wilmore, Kentucky: Asbury Theological Seminary, 1982), p. 18.

[2]*The Appeal to Men of Reason and Religion* and *The Farther Appeal to Men of Reason and Religion* are Wesley's most comprehensive attempts to defend Methodism's place in the Church of England. See Jackson, *Works*, 8:1–247.

[3]Outler, p. 172.

the building. Others defined it within the limits of a particular denomination. Wesley preferred a more general and, in his belief, a more biblical idea. He called the church "a body of people united together in the service of God."[4] As we shall see, he amplified this definition to give it more precise meaning, but his intention was to say that the church is *personal*. He felt that to lose this understanding was to lose the biblical view of the church.

At the same time, Wesley was a realist. Even though he had a broad definition of the church, he knew people would naturally group themselves into particular denominations.[5] He did not believe that this was wrong. He did not try to eliminate distinctions between denominations. The unity he saw and worked for was more a unity of spirit than a unity of structure. Consequently, he had friends and supporters in a wide range of communions. He could move easily among groups as diverse as Roman Catholics and independents. This was due to his fundamental understanding of the church as people.

It is still this personal dimension that attracts people to the church. Surveys have confirmed that most people today are drawn toward the church because of its personal emphases—relational ministries, warm and friendly atmosphere, meaningful fellowship, and a place to form significant friendships. Unfortunately, too many churches lack the personal dimension. Institutionalism takes precedence over individuals. Buildings and budgets seem to be more important than ultimate concerns. These

---

[4]Jackson, *Works*, 6:392 (sermon: "Of the Church").
[5]Ibid., pp. 392–93. Cf. Outler, p. 172.

emphases create a psychology that views the church more as an organization than an organism. When this happens we have lost the foundational attitude that was so important to Wesley.

Wesley affirmed the personal dimension, using Ephesians 4:1–6 as his controlling text. This passage emphasizes the unity of believers. With Paul, Wesley saw the church as one Body, "comprehending not only . . . any one family, not only the Christians of one congregation, of one city, of one province, or nation, but all persons on the face of the earth who answer the character here given."[6] In other words, he believed in the church universal.

Even when the Methodist movement gained momentum, he continued to maintain that his followers were nothing more than Bible Christians. He resolutely stated that they did not divide themselves at all from the living body of Christ, or even from the Church of England.[7] At the same time he did not lose the priority of God's will over the opinions and organizations of men. He wrote, "We will obey the rules and governors of the Church whenever we can, consistently with our duty of God. Whenever we cannot, we will quietly obey God rather than men."[8] This spirit enabled Wesley to exercise an ecumenical spirit, all the while seeking God's will above any human associations. In the final analysis, this is what it means to say that the church is one body.

---

[6]Jackson, *Works*, p. 394.

[7]One of his clearest statements to this effect was "The Character of a Methodist," *Works*, 8:339–47. The conference minutes of 1747 also contain comments of a similar nature; see Outler, p. 172.

[8]Outler, p. 173.

Wesley also affirmed that the church has one Spirit. For him it was the Spirit who "animates . . . all the living members of the Church of God."[9] This idea is crucial, for it makes it plain that Wesley did not equate membership in a church with spiritual vitality. Early in his ministry he encountered those who equated membership and experience. Sermons like "The Circumcision of the Heart" and "Salvation By Faith" fell on stony ground. But Wesley went on, knowing that the Holy Spirit was the "fountain of all spiritual life."[10]

It is important to note that Wesley did not advocate any particular manifestation of the Spirit as necessary proof that one was Spirit filled. His journal documents many extraordinary (even unusual) manifestations.[11] Interestingly, Wesley did not seek to promote or prohibit such occurrences. He was aware that some experiences were counterfeit, but he knew that many were authentic. Time would reveal which were which. In the rapid pace of his ministry Wesley did not feel called to spend an inordinate amount of time judging the response and experience of his hearers.

In our own time the charismatic renewal has matured in this regard. In the earlier days people seemed almost consumed with judging the validity or invalidity of others' experiences. In more recent times the emphasis has switched from particular gifts to the powerful giver of the gifts. Wesley would

---

[9]Jackson, *Works*, 6:394.
[10]Ibid.
[11]Jackson, *Works*, 1:187–97. The first two months (April and May, 1739) of Wesley's field preaching serve as a good example of such manifestations.

rejoice in this. He knew that God works in many ways his wonders to perform. One of the dynamics of revival is that it breaks through stereotypes and deals with people individually. He would call us to promote the Spirit-filled life, but without passing judgment on how such life is to be lived.

Allowing that the church is one body made alive by the one Spirit, Wesley went on to declare that it has one Lord, one faith, and one baptism. For Wesley, the lordship of Christ is the Christian's greatest joy. To live under his lordship provides an experience that he could only describe as "sitting in heavenly places with Christ."[12] But it was not sitting in the passive sense of the term. Christ's lordship calls for our disciplined obedience. This is one reason why Wesley emphasized the means of grace. He knew that personally and corporately we are called to live under Christ's Lordship. No area is outside of his control.

When Wesley said that the church has "one faith," he did not mean a single code of doctrine to which all were bound to subscribe. His own theological position included an indebtedness to Roman Catholic, Lutheran, Reformed, Puritan, and Anglican traditions.[13] In this sense Methodism has always recognized a healthy breadth in belief. The chief criterion for entrance into the United Societies was not a particular theological stance, but "a desire to flee from the wrath to come."[14]

---

[12]Jackson, Works, 6:394.

[13]One of the best works to demonstrate Wesley's indebtedness to a variety of theological traditions is Colin Williams' John Wesley's Theology Today (Nashville: Abingdon, 1960).

[14]John Wesley, The Nature, Design, and General Rules of the United Societies (Newcastle-Upon-Tyne: John Gooding on the Side, 1743), p. 5. Cf. Jackson, Works, 8:270.

Unfortunately, this spirit has been taken to mean that Methodists are theologically indifferent. Wesley's statement, "If thy heart is right as my heart is right, give me thy hand" has been mistakenly used to support contemporary, open-ended pluralism. However, to interpret him this way makes at least three mistakes. First, it overlooks the fact that reputable Wesley scholars have borne witness to his classic orthodoxy.[15] Second, it forgets that Wesley himself stood against trends toward uncritical pluralism[16] in his own day. Third, it blurs the distinction between doctrine and opinion. When Wesley urged his followers to have a "catholic spirit," it is clear from the context that he meant in matters that were nonessential.[17] In the same sermon, in fact, he spoke to those who would equate "catholic spirit" with open-ended pluralism:

> A man of truly catholic spirit has not now his religion to seek. He is fixed as the sun in his judgement concerning the main branches of Christian doctrine. . . . He does not halt between two opinions or vainly try to blend them into one.[18]

This means that when Wesley said that the church has "one faith," he did not have an ambiguous concept of faith in mind. He believed that the fundamental doctrines of Christianity were set forth in Scripture, articulated in the major creeds of the

[15]Outler, p. 92. Cf. Williams, pp. 13–17.

[16]The term for this in the eighteenth century was "speculative latitudinarianism." Wesley stood against this. Cf. *Works*, 8:214.

[17]Ibid., pp. 492–504 (sermon: "Catholic Spirit").

[18]Ibid.

first 450 years of church history,[19] and described in
the Anglican Church's Thirty Nine Articles of Religion. This accounts for his not producing another
creed for the early Methodists in Britain. Rupert
Davies correctly notes that "Wesley, as a practical
man, did not spend time in expounding what had
been perfectly well expounded by others."[20] But let
there be no doubt that he knew and accepted classic
orthodoxy. That he wanted others to do the same is
clear, especially in relation to American Methodists.
When it became clear that the American Methodists
would form a separate denomination, Wesley showed
his concern for content in faith by abridging the
Thirty Nine Articles of the Church of England into
twenty four statements of faith that he expected the
new church to embrace.[21]

The real question for Wesley on the matter of
faith was not content, but rather, "How does faith
operate in the church?" For some it operated as a
test. Persons were admitted into the fellowship of
some churches only if they accepted the particular
statement of faith held by that body. For Wesley,
faith was first *awareness*. It was characterized early
on by repentance. Adherance to the group's doctrine
came later, after faith (as turning from sin to Christ)
was professed. Wesley operated on the premise that
faith must first be existential before it can be con-
ceptual. In this he felt he was following the example

---

[19]Especially the Apostles' and Nicene Creeds.
[20]Rupert Davies, *Methodism* (London: Epworth Press,
1963), p. 82.
[21]These articles can be found in the Book of Discipline of
denominations associated with early Methodism, e.g., the
United Methodist, Free Methodist, Wesleyan Methodist, and
Nazarene Churches.

of the early church, which developed its creeds as an expression of its faith, not a precondition for it. He also felt this approach would guard against creedalism and the "dead orthodoxy" that had characterized too many groups of his day.

This faith was confirmed in "one baptism." Theologically, he saw baptism as bestowing grace, which cleansed one of the guilt of original sin and opened the way to a future of faith and hope in Christ.[22] He saw it not only as a single act, but also as the sign to the church that God is continually bestowing grace upon the body.[23] Wesley did not try to explain how this is done. He was wise enough to leave mystery as mystery, but he did want his people to see baptism as more than a mere symbol. He wanted them to see it as an actual means of grace, as a genuine act of God in the life of the one baptized.

As we have seen, Wesley followed closely the Pauline analogy of the church in the book of Ephesians. He felt this was the biblical answer to the question, "What is the church?" He also believed that Paul's description was harmonious with the nineteenth article of religion in the Anglican Church, which states,

> The visible Church of Christ is a congregation of faithful men, in which the pure word of God is preached, and the sacraments be duly administered.[24]

Wesley recognized that to be this kind of body placed weighty responsibilities upon its members.

---

[22]Jackson, *Works*, 10:188–201.
[23]Ibid., 6:395.
[24]Ibid., p. 396.

This is why discipline was so important to him in the growth of the Methodist Societies. Using Scripture again, he identified these tasks with walking "worthy of the vocation wherewith we are called." This meant thinking, speaking, and acting in every instance in a manner worthy of Christ. Specifically, it meant adopting a spirit of humility and love, striving for the unity of the Spirit in the bond of peace.[25]

Wesley's own words are the best way to summarize his views of the church. Realizing that the church is God's primary vehicle for extending the kingdom until Christ returns, he wrote

> In the mean time, let all those who are real members of the Church, see that they walk holy and unblamable in all things. "Ye are the light of the world!" Ye are " a city set upon a hill' and "cannot be hid." O "let your light shine before men!" Show them your faith by your works. Let them see, by the whole tenor of your conversation, that your hope is all laid up above! Let all your words and actions evidence the spirit whereby you are animated! Above all things, let your love abound. Let it extend to every child of man: Let it overflow to every child of God. By this let all men know whose disciples ye are, because you "love one another."[26]

---

[25]Jackson, *Works*, pp. 398–99.
[26]Ibid., pp. 400–401.

For Discussion

1. What light does Wesley's decision to remain within the Church of England shed on contemporary efforts at church renewal?

2. How do you respond to Wesley's fundamental notion of the church as *personal*? Why does it strike you as it does?

3. How can Wesley's response to differing Christian experiences be a guide for us? Is it sufficient to simply let time show what is authentic and what is not? What other criteria, if any, would you want to add?

4. In an age of pluralism it is not easy to have an open spirit and a clear commitment to orthodoxy. How can the Wesleyan emphasis here be applied today? In your experience, which side of the coin needs more emphasis—openness of spirit or commitment to orthodoxy? Why?

For Further Reading

Sermon, "Of the Church" *Works*, 6:392–401.

Sermon, "On Schism" *Works*, 6:401–10.

Sermon, "On Attending the Church Service" *Works*, 6:174–85.

Almost the whole of volume 10 of the *Works* is devoted to Wesley's view of the church and the place of the early Methodist movement in the larger body of Christ.

Renewal—
the Wesley Way

A new look at the Eighteenth Century period of renewal in the church's history could shed some light on the need that we face in the church today.

Samuel Emerick

10
Renewal—the Wesley Way

J ohn Wesley was a true son of the Reformation. He
would affirm with Luther and Calvin that the
church is continually being renewed. He believed
Methodism was one of the primary means God had
ordained in the eighteenth century to bring revival to
the church.[1] We can be sure that he would support
contemporary efforts at church renewal, and he
would want those in the Wesleyan tradition to be in
the forefront of such concerns.

However, the question remains, "What kind of
renewal are we seeking? How can we know if we are
on the right track?" It is my conviction that we can
learn much from John Wesley in the matter of church
renewal.[2] As this book comes to a close, I would like
to propose some principles for renewal which grow
out of a study of Wesley's ministry and the early
Methodist movement. I want to try to answer the
question, "How would John Wesley seek to renew
the church if he were alive today?"

First, he would urge all people to personally

---

[1]Jackson, *Works*, 8:299.
[2]Cf. Howard Snyder's, *The Radical Wesley* (Downers Grove:
Inter-Varsity, 1980).

experience Christ. It had not been without intense struggle that Wesley came to see the centrality of a personal faith in Christ. His heart-warming experience at Aldersgate became the motivating purpose of his life. Justification by faith became the touchstone of the Methodist revival, and Wesley preached this theme on every conceivable occasion.[3]

Believing as he did in the necessity of personal faith, Wesley urged it upon persons who were already members of the Church of England. To his surprise, the message fell on deaf ears. To them the notion of personally experiencing God smacked of "enthusiasm."[4] So pulpits began closing to him. But rather than compromise what he knew to be scriptural truth, Wesley continued to preach it. He moved into the open air and preached "the glad tidings of salvation" to those who were open to the message. It was in this context that the revival began, and the theme of personal salvation was its hallmark.

It seems amazing that it would even be necessary to make this the first principle for contemporary church renewal. But the fact remains that the message of personal salvation is not going forth consistently in the church. During the last fifteen years I have rarely, if ever, heard lay persons testify to hearing a call to personal commitment to Christ. I realize that many of them sat under such preaching without it making a conscious impression, but the whole matter cannot be written off that easily. Too many churches have settled into a moralistic view of Christianity that is fundamentally humanistic rather

---

[3]Outler, p. 197.

[4]"Enthusiasm" was a negative term in the eighteenth century, roughly synonymous with our term "fanaticism."

than Christocentric. The emphasis is on being good
and doing good, but with little emphasis on the
power to accomplish this kind of living. In this respect we are not unlike the sleepy Anglicans whom
Wesley sought to awaken.[5] We can be sure that John
Wesley would do all within his power to advance the
preaching of personal faith in Christ.

Second, Wesley would urge Christians to greater
degrees of discipline. In a very real sense, his whole
life was an example of Christian discipline. The par-
sonage years at Epworth grounded him in the fun-
damentals of discipline. The Oxford years, especially after 1725, served only to give further shape to
his disciplined life. In Georgia, Wesley maintained a
pace that would have broken most men. His diary
records that for over sixty years Wesley lived a re-
markably disciplined life.

In 1778, Wesley preached an interesting sermon
entitled, "The Work of God in North America." It
was his attempt to relate the various dispensations of
divine providence in the American colonies as far
back as 1736. In the sermon, Wesley commented on
the preaching of George Whitefield, which has been
acknowledged as a contributing factor to the first
Great Awakening in America. Wesley noted that on
Whitefield's last journey to America the evangelist
lamented that many had drawn back unto perdition.
In a telling statement Wesley sought to account for
their decline:

> And what wonder? For it was a true
> saying, which was common in the ancient

---

[5]One of Wesley's most effective sermons was entitled,
"Awake Thou that Sleepest." Cf. Jackson, *Works,* 5:25–36.

> church, "The soul and the body make a
> man; and the spirit and discipline make a
> Christian." But those who were more or
> less affected by Mr. Whitefield's preach-
> ing had no discipline at all. They had no
> shadow of discipline; nothing of the kind.
> They were formed into no societies. They
> had no Christian connection with each
> other, nor were ever taught to watch over
> each other's souls. So that if they fell into
> lukewarmness, or even into sin, he had
> none to lift him up. He might fall lower
> and lower, yea, into hell, if he would; for
> who regarded it?[6]

Hardly any quotation from Wesley is more in-
sightful than this; it clearly shows his feeling about
the necessity for discipline in the Christian life. Yet,
this attitude can be easily misunderstood in our time
when "hang loose" has come to replace "shape up"
as a guiding principle. Three facts need to be mentioned to enforce and interpret Wesley's idea.

The first is theological. Discipline is essential
because of humanity's "bent to sinning." If we are
left to ourselves to merely "do our own thing" and
"go with the flow", we will shun the disciplined life.
Christian maturity is not automatic, it must be culti-
vated. Discipline is the means of that cultivation.

Second, Wesley's insistence on discipline must
not be viewed in a narrow, legalistic, or even cultic
sense. It is too easy (and wrong) to read into these
remarks the demands of a spiritual dictator who re-
quired a set course of action from his followers. It

---

[6]Jackson, *Works,* 7:411 (sermon: "The Work of God in North
America").

must be remembered that Wesley spoke of discipline first in terms of principles. The rules for the United Societies are based upon principles that Wesley believed to be scriptural and in keeping with the practices of the early church. To a large extent, he left the particularization of those principles up to the various societies. The specific disciplines he recommended were those that had been well tested in the history of the church. His was no novel or faddish approach to discipline. It is important to see Wesley's views as those of a benevolent spiritual director who knew the basic principles and best expressions of the disciplined life.

Third, Wesley's discipline was all-encompassing. He did not major on minors, or get hung up in the minutae of the disciplined life. The goal for Wesley was holiness, which he called "the fulness of faith." The outcome was not this or that particular expression, but rather the renewal of the image of God.[7] In order for this transformation to take place, Wesley knew that nothing less than the consecration of one's entire self to God would suffice. He trusted the individual, in cooperation with the Holy Spirit, to work out the specifics of that consecration. When Wesley's commitment to discipline is seen in this light, it is clear why such a spirit must be at the heart of any significant renewal today.

A third Wesleyan principle for renewal would be the getting together of believers in groups. It was by proclamation that Wesley sought to extend the kingdom. By the societies he sought to mature it. These twin activities formed the heart of early

[7]Outler, p. 28.

Methodist evangelism. As the years went by, Wesley began to observe some deterioration in the group structure. He warned against it in the strongest terms:

> Never omit meeting your Class or Band; never absent yourself from any public meeting. These are the very sinews of our Society; and whatever weakens or tends to weaken our regard for these, or our exactness in attending them, strikes at the very root of our community. . . . The private weekly meetings for prayer, examination, and particular exhortation has been the greatest means of keeping and confirming every blessing that was received by the word preached and diffusing it to others. . . . Without this religious connection and intercourse the most ardent attempts, by mere preaching, have proved no lasting use.[8]

In terms of contemporary church growth, Wesley was ahead of his time in realizing the potential in group ministries. However, he was only drawing on the resources of a principle that went back into the earliest Christian church.[9] A fruitful study awaits anyone who will examine Wesley's bands, classes, and societies searching for contemporary connections and relationship with small-group dynamics.

How can we square this emphasis of Wesley's with the many churches in the Wesleyan tradition who limit corporate ministries to church school and public worship? We cannot. The lack of relational

---

[8]Jackson, Works, 11:433.
[9]Cf. Acts 2:46; 5:42, Rom. 16:5.

ministries in the church has contributed signifi-
cantly to a lost of spiritual vitality. God has not
designed that the members of the church should
function individually. Dependence, mutual responsibility, and corporate nurture are at the heart of
what it means to be the church. To be sure, group
experiences can become perfunctory and they have
their own problems. But to omit them from the ongoing life of the body of Christ is to work against
time-honored patterns of renewal and to lose the
Wesleyan spirit in this important area.

Fourth, Wesley would call us to a renewed appreciation for the sacraments. As previously shown,
he saw them as divinely instituted means for con-
veying grace to people. His views on both baptism
and the Lord's Supper clearly raised them above the
level of mere symbols and gave them a potency to
effect changes in the lives of people.[10] Baptism
(while not identical with new birth or regeneration)
did convey grace to cleanse one of the guilt of original sin and infuse a principle of grace "which will
not be wholly taken away unless we quench the Holy
Spirit of God by long continued wickedness."[11] The
Lord's Supper was ordained of God to convey "either
preventing, or justifying, or sanctifying grace, ac-
cording to (our) several necessities."[12]

The sacraments were an important way for
people to continually remember the objectivity of
Christianity. It is *of grace*, not of ourselves that we

---

[10]Two representative treatises are "On Baptism" (Works,
10:188–201) and "The Duty of Constant Communion"
(7:147–57).

[11]Jackson, Works, p. 192.

[12]Ibid., 1:280.

are what we are. The sacraments were constant reminders of this truth. Because early Methodism did stress personal experience (conversion, assurance, sanctification, etc.), it was all the more important to keep this objective balance before the people.

We may be sure that Wesley would call us to "sacramental renewal," and get a new vision of the power of these means of grace. He would call us to be present on all occasions when the sacraments are administered, especially Communion. He would urge congregations to administer the Lord's Supper frequently.[13] He would want us to believe that God desires to bring about renewal through the sacraments now as throughout the ages of church history.

A fifth principle for renewal is Wesley's emphasis that Christ be offered to everyone. Wesley never let the Methodist movement become his only concern. He constantly kept the needs of the larger church and the nation at heart. He believed that Methodism was one way God had chosen to bring a cure to the sickness of society. The varied ministries of the Foundry in London illustrate his concern for the whole gospel. There he carried on a full-orbed preaching and discipling ministry, operated a medical dispensary, ran a bookstore, organized a school for children, and provided a shelter for widows (one of whom was his own mother). He had a particular concern for the poor, feeling that English aristocracy had abandoned them.[14] There is no doubt that he

---

[13]Evidence from early Methodism would seem to suggest at least a weekly observance of the Lord's Supper.

[14]Cf. Maldwyn Edwards, *John Wesley and the Eighteenth Century: A Study of His Social and Political Influence* (London: Epworth Press, 1955).

would exhort us never to forget that the world is still our parish.

In our own time the cause of social concerns goes under many names and grows out of differing philosophies. It is important to understand Wesley's social contribution in light of the ideologies that promote social reform today. The key for doing so is the remembrance that Wesley's social concern was inextricably rooted in the Christian faith. He was fundamentally an earnest Christian, who sought through a variety of means to effect the redemption of fallen humanity.[15] For this reason Wesley cannot be used as a support for Communism, Marxism, or any other "ism" that has at its heart an atheistic pre-supposition. Nothing in his social concern can be identified with destructive or violent expressions of revolution espoused by some revolutionary movements today. His was the power of love and compassion, working *within* a society that had its share of injustices. The testimony of some historians that the Wesleyan revival was the greatest force for social change in the eighteenth century is a testimony to the legitimacy of *Christian* methods to evoke transformation. It calls into question any movement that divorces itself from a Christian motif and acts as if the end justifies the means. Wesley would call us to a ministry to the total person in the total society, all over the world. But he would always stress the need for such ministry to be distinctively related to the name and spirit of Christ.

Obviously these are only some of the principles

---

[15]Cf. chap. 7, Henry Bett, *The Spirit of Methodism* (London: Epworth Press, 1937).

for renewal that are exemplified in the life and ministry of John Wesley. I am convinced that these principles are timeless. They stand at the heart of authentic Christianity, ancient or modern. If we use the term "Methodist" in any sense comparable to the way Wesley used it, we cannot ignore these principles. If we do ignore them, we may still call ourselves Methodists, but our founding father would not know us. If we apply them, God will bless us and give life to that portion of His body known as Methodism.

For Discussion

1. Which of the renewal strategies mentioned in this chapter seems to be the most important for your church? Why?
2. What expressions of lay ministry do you have in your church?
3. How can the church today call people to discipline without falling prey to a legalistic spirit?
4. What values do you see in having another Christian, or group of Christians, with whom you can share your experience?

For Further Reading

George Hunter, *The Contagious Congregation* (Nashville: Abingdon, 1979).

Albert Outler, *Evangelism in the Wesleyan Spirit* (Nashville: Tidings, 1971).

Howard Snyder, *The Radical Wesley* (Downers Grove: Inter-Varsity, 1980).

A Basic
Bibliography
for Wesley Studies

A Basic Bibliography
for Wesley Studies

The following primary and secondary materials are intended to lead you into further study of Wesley's life and thought. The primary material contains the major works of Wesley in their most recognized editions. Note that several have been recently reprinted and are currently available. The secondary material is intentionally limited to material that is relatively easy to find in many colleges, seminaries, larger public libraries, and some Christian bookstores. Most of the entries are annotated to tell something of their content and significance. A number of them contain useful bibliographies that can lead to further reading. It is my hope that you will continue to familiarize yourself with Wesley through these resources.

PRIMARY MATERIAL

Baker, Frank. ed. *The Works of John Wesley.* Oxford: Oxford University Press, 1976, 34 vols. This is the new, definitive edition, superior to the Jackson edition listed below. However it is coming out slowly, a volume at a time.

Curnock, Nehemiah. ed. *The Journal of John Wesley.* London: Epworth, 1938, 8 vols. This is the standard edition of Wesley's journal. It also contains Curnock's transcription of Wesley's unpublished diaries.

Jackson, Thomas. ed. *The Works of John Wesley* Grand Rapids: Baker, 1979, 14 vols. This is the best available set of Wesley's works. Until the Oxford Press edition is complete, it will remain the major resource for studying Wesley.

Sugden, E.H., ed. *The Standard Sermons of John Wesley* London: Epworth, 1956, 2 vols. Sugden's annotations are helpful in more fully understanding the sermons Wesley selected to serve as doctrinal standards for Methodism.

Telford, John. ed. *The Letters of John Wesley* London: Epworth, 1964, 8 vols. Until the volumes of letters in the Oxford Press edition of Wesley's works are completed, this edition will continue to be the best source of studying Wesley's correspondence.

Wesley, John. *Explanatory Notes Upon the New Testament* Grand Rapids: Baker 1982. These notes, together with the standard sermons and Articles of Religion comprise the historic doctrinal standards of Methodism.

_____. *Explanatory Notes Upon the Old Testament* Salem, OH: Schmul 1975, 3 vols. This set completed Wesley's attempt to provide inexpensive, annotated versions of the Scriptures for the early Methodists.

SECONDARY MATERIAL

Ayling, Stanley. *John Wesley* Nashville: Abingdon, 1979. This work is composed by a British biographer who is not himself a Methodist. It is basically a good work, but the author lacks familiarity with Wesleyan thought at some points.

Cannon, William R. *The Theology of John Wesley* Nashville: Abingdon, 1946. This is one of the best theologies of Wesley produced in the twentieth century.

Green, V.H.H. *The Young Mr. Wesley* London: Edward Arnold, 1961. No published work treats the years 1725–34 better than this one.

Mickey, Paul. *Essentials of Wesleyan Theology* Grand Rapids: Zondervan, 1980. This work utilizes a contemporary affirmation of faith to describe Wesley's theology. It sets Wesley in mainstream classic Protestantism, often comparing him with Luther and Calvin.

Outler, Albert, *John Wesley* Oxford: University Press, 1964. This work is primarily excerpts from Wesley coupled with excellent introductions by Dr. Outler.

_____. *Theology in the Wesleyan Spirit* Nashville: Discipleship Resources, 1975. A lay-oriented work treating the major tenets of Wesley's theology.

Rowe, Kenneth, ed. *The Place of Wesley in the Christian Tradition* Metuchen, NJ: Scarecrow Press, 1976. An excellent collection of essays showing Wesley's relation to other traditions. The book contains one of the best bibliographies on Wesley studies in print.

Schmidt, Martin. *John Wesley: A Theological Biography*, 3 vols. Nashville: Abingdon, 1960. One of the best and most comprehensive presentations of Wesley's life and thought.

Tuttle, Robert. *John Wesley: His Life and Theology* Grand Rapids: Zondervan, 1978. This work treats Wesley using an appealing first-person style, as if Wesley himself were speaking.

Williams, Colin. *John Wesley's Theology Today* Nashville: Abingdon, 1960. One of the finest contemporary interpretations of Wesley's theology.